The
promise
of HOPE

The
promise
of HOPE

Coping When Life Caves In

WILLIAM M. KINNAIRD

Stephen Ministries • St. Louis, Missouri

The Promise of Hope

1994 edition published as part of the Care Classics® Series by Stephen Ministries. Copyright © 1993 by William M. Kinnaird, previously ISBN 0-687-34330-5. All rights reserved. This edition licensed by permission of William M. Kinnaird. 1981 edition published by Abingdon.

ISBN 1-930445-03-2

Library of Congress Catalog Card Number 81-3599

Printed in the United States of America

12
06

Dedication

I dedicated the original edition of this book to two persons: Paul Tournier and my daughter Elleanor. Since then Dr. Tournier has left us, but his memory still remains powerfully with me. As much as any human, he is and was my beloved mentor. His wisdom and compassion were a model for the man I'd like to be.

My daughter has now grown up, married, and has a wonderful life of her own. She and I have had to work through many things to build and maintain a solid relationship. Our efforts are testimony to something I believe with all my heart: To have a healthy relationship, each person in it needs to be open and honest and forgiving. Repression of thoughts and feelings gets you nowhere.

I'd also like to dedicate this edition to two dear friends I did not know when the original edition was published: George Wirth and Jerry Wright, both pastors at my church, First Presbyterian of Atlanta. They are far more than pastors to me; they are my friends in every sense of the word. They are models of what I wish we saw more of in the churches today: open minds and open hearts. To George and Jerry, I love you both very much and treasure your friendship.

Is it not you, O Lord our God?
We set our hope on you,
for it is you who do all this.

—Jeremiah 14:22b (NRSV)

Contents

Introduction

Have you ever prized a book over time, perhaps even regularly recommending it to friends, only to discover that it is out of print? Have you ever loaned a favorite book and then forgotten to whom you loaned it? When you went to buy another copy, you discovered to your dismay that it was out of print.

Stephen Ministries is giving new life to some well-loved books with its Care Classic® Series. Books in this series are high quality resources, theologically sound yet eminently practical and immediately applicable to daily living. They fill a definite need for individuals and congregations of all Christian denominations who are seeking quality resources to equip God's people for the work of ministry.

The Promise of Hope, the second release in this series, is a book I have referred to many times through the years. I first met Bill Kinnaird in 1982 and read this book shortly thereafter. I am impressed by his robust sense of humor and profound insights into the ministry of caring. The partnership between Bill and Stephen Ministries in republishing this excellent title gives many more readers the opportunity to learn and grow from his insights and honest sharing.

This book practicalizes caring. In sharing his deepest thoughts and personal experiences, Bill Kinnaird tells and shows how best to care for others. Through the author's eyes, readers learn to discern the depth of a person's hurt and what caring in Christ really means. Each day more and more individuals know the pain of severed relationships, terminal illnesses, and other challenges of life. Think of the impact quality Christian caring can have—and is having—on our broken world. This is Bill's valuable contribution toward that reality.

I thank God for Bill's courage and commitment to Jesus Christ. I believe what you learn from *The Promise of Hope* will remain with you for a long time to come.

Kenneth C. Haugk
Executive Director
Stephen Ministries

Preface

A psychologist friend of mine says, "Speak in growing terms. If you speak in arrival terms, you are the harbinger of your own disaster."

I can relate to that. I know I have not arrived. I'm still growing. I'm convinced I will be as long as I'm on this earth. I'm convinced that Christ's admonition, "Be ye perfect," was a call to get on the road to perfection. It was not a command to be perfect overnight. I know of no perfect human beings, although I know of some beautiful ones who are far beyond me in their journey to wholeness and perfection.

All I can do is tell you about my continuing journey. I have my struggles. I have my ups and downs. I am not (most assuredly not!) perfect. I am on the road. I am growing.

I have shared some of my experiences, and the insights I've gained on the journey, in *Joy Comes with the Morning*. Here are some more. I trust they will encourage you and that you will find, as I have, the promise of hope.

Prologue

The Call in the Middle of the Night

It was 4:00 A.M. I hadn't slept at all. I'd been lying there for hours. A Holiday Inn in the middle of the night can be the loneliest place in the world.

In those days motels didn't have chaplains on call twenty-four hours a day. There was nobody but God and me—and I wasn't so sure God was there. I desperately wanted to hear the sound of a human voice—somebody who would tell me it was okay, that I could survive another "dark night of the soul."

I dialed Suicide Prevention. I wasn't very close to suicide then, but I came much closer in the ensuing weeks and months. My wife of ten and a half years had just told me she wanted a divorce. My life—or at least life as I had known it—had come to a crushing end. I was desperate; the pain was unbearable. I didn't think I could go on. I needed a human voice to tell me I could.

But I needed more than that—much more. I needed the reassurance that there was a God out there someplace, who not only knew me by name, but who would also act in my behalf. I needed to know that God had a plan for my life.

Larry's voice was at the other end of the line. He was the suicide prevention counselor on duty that night. "Do you believe in God?" I tentatively asked him.

15

Larry's devastating reply was, "No, you are your own god."

I don't remember any more of the conversation—if indeed there was any. I was in a state of shock. I may have hung up without saying another word. There was nothing more *to* say, and there was certainly nothing more to hear. Larry didn't have the answer; he didn't have the words of support and encouragement I desperately needed.

But my story doesn't end there, as well it might. If I had believed what Larry told me, I wouldn't be writing this true story. I might even be dead.

Somehow I didn't believe Larry. Even though many times later I felt great despair and depression, I never entirely gave up hope that there was a God. What I had trouble believing was that God would, or could, do anything about my situation. A God who is just out there someplace, but who doesn't help in times of trouble, isn't a very comforting God and he isn't a God I can love.

Fortunately for me, Larry didn't have the last word. I met other people—beautiful Christian people—who not only told me there is a God, but who also demonstrated God's great love. They told me God loves me and Jesus Christ has a plan for my life. They told me that if I would commit my life to him and ask him to take it over, he would. They said this with assurance because that had happened in their lives.

I made that commitment in the summer of 1971. I would like to tell you that once I made it, all my problems were solved, my marriage was restored, and I have lived in idyllic bliss on a mountaintop ever since. That would not be true. I have lived through many dark nights of the soul since. The remarriage of my ex-wife in 1977 was an even more crushing blow than the divorce six years earlier. I had never completely given up hope that there would be a reconciliation. The remarriage destroyed that hope.

But I can tell you—and in all honesty—there *is* a God. Larry was wrong. And I can tell you that the Bible portrays God accurately as a God who acts. God has worked in my life, and continues to work until this day. God, through Jesus Christ, has given me a purpose and meaning and joy where there was only total blackness. God has made my life a radiant and glorious adventure.

Recently I was with a man who knew me well in the midst of my darkest night. He and his wife took me into their home at that time to love and nourish me, as I desperately needed help. He said the other day, "When people ask me, 'You don't really believe all that stuff about Jesus Christ, do you?' I tell them, 'Well, I knew Bill Kinnaird when he was dead; and he is alive today. That's enough for me to go on.'"

If you ever call me in the middle of the night and ask if there is a God, I won't give you the same answer Larry gave me. I have learned through the faithfulness of Jesus Christ that there is a God who delights in restoring broken people to wholeness. That for me is the promise of hope.

1

Embrace the Hurt

"God has given my life a purpose and meaning and joy by changing it from total blackness to a radiant and glorious adventure."

Those words describe the change in my life. But I do not mean to imply by them that I am now immune to pain, hurt, and suffering. Part of my life now involves learning to handle the hurts that tend to get me down.

I remember a down time in my life—one of many. I had just put my two daughters on a plane and sent them three thousand miles away from me. I knew it would be five months or more before I would see them again. The anticipation of sending them out of my life yet another time almost spoiled for me their short, one-week visit. I tried not to let my hurt show through, but I'm not very good at covering up my emotions. Normally I'm a joyous, outgoing person. Yet around my own daughters I have not always been that way. Sometimes I have tried to *force* it, and we can never force our feelings. Sometimes I have tried to hide my true feelings when I'm around them, and I'm not a very good actor.

I've learned that children gravitate *to* joy and *away* from sadness and gloom. As John Claypool once said, they naturally gravitate to the most joyous person in their constellation. He told of his fun-loving uncle who took him to his first state fair when he was six. The uncle introduced the young lad to the wonder of cotton candy and in the process became an idol and a revered hero.

That's the kind of father I've always wanted to be for my children. I think I was once, and I basically am that kind of father. But we have many facets to our personalities, and different circumstances trigger different emotions. Being apart from children I so deeply love has often triggered emotions with which I am not comfortable.

Even my own writings haven't always helped. I read what I have written (and truly felt at a particular time) and almost wonder that I am the same person who could say and feel all those joyous things. But I'm not being a hypocrite. I've actually had those joyous moments, those victories over deep despair while in the midst of it.

When I'm in a down time, I pray those moments will come again. History tells me they will. I started to say, "My faith in God tells me they will." But that would be hypocritical. My faith doesn't always tell me that. I can look back, though, at many hours of despair and know that, so far, I have come through each one of them, by the grace of God, I am sure. I believe God is on my side.

But how do I handle my hurt, my pain? That's the question. I could give you (and myself) a lot of pious platitudes. They would only be words, and I don't want to do that. I want to be honest.

One morning just after my daughters had visited me, as I came out of the shower dripping wet, the phone was ringing. It was a friend—a fairly new friend—yet an "old" one too, whom I had met at a conference four months previously. She served as interpreter for a memorable visit with Paul Tournier, a Swiss counselor and author who became a revered mentor, and helped the two of us bridge the language barrier through the bond of love. She knew my feelings about my children and the lack of peace in my heart, and she had asked God to give her some wisdom to share with me. She wrote down the thoughts that came to her .

One of them was: "Embrace the hurt." In other words, I should accept it and not try to change it by my own efforts. "You wouldn't be the person you are," she said, "without the hurt you have already suffered. This new hurt can help you be God's hands and feet to help other hurting people."

I totally agreed with her counsel. How to put it into practice, however, was an entirely different matter.

How do we embrace hurt? How do we accept it? How do we, as Catherine Marshall wrote so frequently, relinquish hurt or a desired ambition? How do we surrender it?

A psychologist friend of mine told me I must surrender to God some deep emotions and longings. How do I do that? My friend on the phone said I need to surrender even my love for my children. How do I do that?

I'd like to sum up this chapter with a word of hope,

but I insist on not being a hypocrite. I don't want to say what I don't honestly feel. Yet history does tell me that God has been faithful and has been my deliverer in times past.

What would I do without a belief in a God who acts? What do people in deep trouble do without any faith? I think the answer is many don't make it. They end up on skid row, in mental institutions, or at the end of a rope, literally or figuratively. They try to numb the hurt with alcohol or drugs or promiscuity. Anything to kill the pain. I know that feeling. I can relate to it. I have experienced it.

Yet at many times in my life the resolve to trust God once again has slowly seeped back into my psyche. I have been able to embrace the hurt and thereby gain inward peace in spite of outward circumstances. And by sharing that with you, maybe—with God's help—I can help you.

2

I've Been There Too

Nobody is more helpful than one who can both say and live out, "I understand, and I love you." During a dark night of the soul in my life, I shared with such a friend who understood and who continued to love. She helped me tremendously. She told me that when she was going through circumstances similar to mine, she shouted at the Lord to do something about the problem or to sustain her in it. God promises to be our sustenance, and in her case, certainly was.

I told her how I had been crying out to God. I also told her that I really wondered if I should be leading a Discipleship Growth Group for a dozen men at our church. I said I didn't have it all put together myself, so I probably shouldn't be trying to lead others. She said people who realize their own inadequacies and failings make the best teachers, not the ones who think they have it all put together.

One of our pastors said during a meeting that none of us really has it all put together. He told of an outstanding man in the church who had shared with a group that he was struggling with problems in his own life and experiencing deep feelings of inadequacy. The pastor said this was one of the most meaningful witnesses he had ever heard. Hearing this, I realized I wasn't alone in feeling I didn't have it all put together—and that it was okay.

I learned that my efforts, even my so-called good ones, were trivial. I couldn't lead a Discipleship Growth Group thinking I had it all put together. I could only lead knowing there was One who did. That One would be the real leader, not me. My friend was able to help me see this and comfort me because she had been there.

3

"You Shouldn't Feel That Way"

I can't think of a more useless thing to tell a suffering person than "you shouldn't feel that way." The point is, he or she does. The "shouldn't" or "should" doesn't change the way a person actually feels, but does often make him or her feel guilty.

I received a letter at a down time in my life from a psychologist friend who said, "I grieve with you over the remarriage of your wife. The pain and grief are inexpressible, I am sure." And he signed his letter "Your friend." I can't explain it, but his letter eased the pain some. It made me feel better. If he had said, "You shouldn't feel that way," I would have felt just that much worse—and angry too.

Another thing that helped me was the realization that God knew me and was also my friend. I knew God cared for me regardless of how I felt and would help me whether or not I had the feelings I "should" have had. I knew God had worked in my life so beautifully and so often in the past, and would do so in the present and future as well.

I think the greatest consolation in a time of despair is the knowledge that God *has* worked in our lives. Until we reach that stage (and none of us is there until a time of trial, until God has rescued us), the best thing that can happen to us is to have loving Christian friends in whose lives God has worked. Through their loyalty (to us and to God), they will hang in there with us and give us the assurance that our God is a God who works, even in the most hopeless situations.

I know I couldn't have gotten through that terrible time in my life without God. But I did get through it. My feelings had nothing to do with it. Jesus Christ had everything to do with it.

4

On Being Understood

The key to understanding is looking at life from the other person's point of view. As Irvin Yalom says in his book *The Theory and Practice of Group Psychotherapy,*[1] "When people begin to understand the other's experiential world, past and present, and view the other's position from his frame of reference, they may begin to understand that the other's point of view may be as appropriate for him as their own is for themselves."

Eugene Kennedy says in his book *The Pain of Being Human,*[2] "If shedding each other's blood makes us enemies, sharing each other's fears makes us brothers. . . . The present tensions only become unbearable when we sentence each other to suffer alone."

I think the greatest expression of love for another is to say, in words or actions, "I understand. I understand *why* you acted as you did. I'm not going to judge you. I'm not saying I would have done any differently if I had been you."

Keith Miller wrote a best seller entitled *Please Love Me.* An equally good title might be *Please Understand*

Me. I believe I could write such a book. Maybe this is it. I have felt most deeply loved when I have been understood. And I have been very frustrated and hurt, even angry, when I have felt misunderstood.

I know it is not always easy to understand other people. But we can always have that as our goal. We can work to discern where they are coming from, what their background is, what their perception might be, how it is to look at life through their eyes. I like the American Indian prayer: "Great Spirit, help me not to judge another man until I have walked in his moccasins one month."

In life we *all* need someone to share not only our fears, but also our joys and our burdens. To use a common slang expression, we need somebody to "dig" us. I hope none of us is sentenced to walk alone. I hope we haven't so sentenced anybody else.

5

Encouraging Words

Out of deep hurt and agonizing loneliness, I once called the hot line of a Presbyterian church in a city in which I was on a business trip. I wanted to talk to someone. I was away from my own pastors and friends, and I'm not so sure I would have called them anyway. I felt I still had some pride left, and I probably wouldn't have wanted them to know I could still feel down. I'd been mostly up for a long time.

I feel the Lord must have blessed that call and anointed the anonymous listener with a special outpouring of the Holy Spirit. What he told me helped me greatly, mainly because of what he didn't tell me. He didn't tell me to quit wallowing in self-pity or to stop feeling sorry for myself. I knew that already. I didn't need to be told. That would have driven me even deeper into despair and perhaps even resentment. You know the story of Job's four friends who chastised him. This man wasn't like them.

What he said was, "I sense a great strength in you. . . . You are looking to and relying on God. You're out doing something for others instead of thinking about yourself all the time."

That certainly wasn't what I was feeling that morning. I was being a hypocrite, I said, since in my writing I tell *others* to be encouraged because of what Christ can and will do. But I wasn't taking my own advice.

I can't repeat the rest of the conversation verbatim, but I came away from it with a sense of renewed hope and even deeper faith. At the end of the conversation, after he asked to pray for me and did so beautifully, I told him how much he had helped me by seizing on my strengths instead of my weaknesses. I suspect he had been trained that way.

We can all take a clue from this wise counselor. We will help others by finding their strengths instead of their sometimes all too apparent weaknesses. I once heard a man say, "It takes ten 'atta-boys' to make up for one 'you jerk.'" I think that may be low on the affirmation side. The put-downs run pretty deep and stay with us a long, long time. And it's even worse when we start putting ourselves down. After all, God doesn't.

6

Only One Answer

There is only one answer to any deep problem—
Jesus Christ. I say that not from theory but from personal
experience.

On my son's tenth birthday, a suicide prevention
counselor told me that he thought the odds were 60-40 I
would take my own life. Thank God the prognostication
didn't come true. I've already mentioned another suicide
prevention counselor who told me that there isn't any
God. "You are your own god," he said. Neither of these
counselors proved the slightest bit helpful. Neither
helped my despair. Neither gave me a reason to live.

A person in such deep despair that he or she is con-
sidering suicide desperately needs a reason to live. That
person needs hope. And there is only one legitimate hope
in such dire circumstances. It isn't ourselves. We *can't*
"straighten up" or "pull ourselves together." We're too
helpless. The lack of hope has taken too much of a toll.
We can't function to help ourselves.

I once talked to a clinical psychologist who told me
he could tell when a person was depressed because that

person would always say to any constructive suggestion, "That won't work." A depressed person has all the answers as to why nothing in this whole wide world is going to prove helpful.

If you know such a person desperately in need of hope but not able to find it, or if you are such a person yourself, let me tell you there *is* hope. There is Jesus Christ. He came to give us hope. He came to mend the broken-hearted, to lift our spirits, to turn us away from despair and hopelessness to himself.

I tell you this because I have *experienced* it. I have seen my life turn from one of total hopelessness to one of great joy and meaning (though not without problems and heartaches). One thing—and one thing only—kept me going through that long, dark period. It was the hope that Jesus Christ just *might* help. He just *might* work one of those miracles other people said he could. He just *might* answer my prayers and those of so many others who fervently prayed for me and hung in there with me and loved me when I wasn't very lovable.

Jesus did. But not always in the way I wanted. He hasn't given me some things I so desperately wanted. But he gives me much, much more. He strengthens my faith. He lets me get to know him personally. He brings so many beautiful people into my life who love me and whom I love. He opens doors of opportunity and service. He excites my intellect. You've heard the expression "An idle mind is the devil's workshop." Well, Jesus never lets my mind be idle. He fills it to overflowing with exciting concepts and ideas. He places before me books and authors who reveal more and more of the wonder and grace and majesty of the almighty God to me. I am desperately in love with Jesus, God's own Son, who revitalizes my life and gives me hope and meaning where there once was none.

This wasn't something those suicide prevention counselors could do for me. They had no personal experience with the living God, or else they would have told me about it. I feel sorry for them, and even sorrier for those poor, unfortunate people they counsel who might end up taking their own lives.

There is a 100-0 chance for us to live, if we will only take it. There *is* a living God who loves us. We will still have heartaches. We will still have problems. But through it all, we have a faithful comforter. We are able to make it. We are not alone.

That is the Christian life. I tell you with every ounce of conviction I have, there *is* hope for even the most hopeless situation. There is hope because Jesus Christ lives.

7

Pure Motives

Do we need pure motives in order to follow God? Do we have to come to a place where all our reasons for wanting God in our lives are the "right" ones? Must we be totally unselfish in everything we do in our Christian life?

I don't think so. I need God in my life *because* of my selfishness. I know my own sin and weakness so well. I know that without God, there would be no way I could cope. Therefore, a part of my reason for following God is selfish rather than unselfish. I *need* God—desperately!

There's more to it than that. God is the one I love and want to follow. I am very grateful for all God has done for me—and continues to do. I don't want to turn my back on someone who has been that kind to me.

But I'll have to confess my motives are tainted. The bottom line for me is I know what my life was without Christ, and I know what it is with him. Simply put, there is no comparison.

When we get down to it, we are all selfish. Why do we want to get to heaven? Isn't it because heaven is the best place? The alternative is certainly not very appealing, to say the least. Some of Jesus' closest disciples even squabbled over who would have the best place in heaven and would be seated closest to their Master. That sounds very selfish to me.

How many of us could be as unselfish as Moses and Paul, who were willing to give up their own places in heaven if others could be saved? Would you do that? Would I? That is as unselfish a position as I could possibly imagine—a willingness even to go to hell so that someone else could go to heaven. If all our motives were required to be that pure, heaven would indeed be a sparsely populated place.

In C. S. Lewis' fairy tale *The Horse and His Boy,* both the young boy Shasta and the girl Aravis ended up as followers of Aslan (Christ). Yet their motives in the beginning were not so pure. Shasta ran away from a bad home situation, and Aravis from an unwanted marriage. They didn't set out with the intention of following Christ. That just developed along the way—and with a lot of nudging patience from Aslan.

I think this is also true with a lot of us. It has certainly been that way with me. I didn't set out on the journey toward Christ because of my purity and unselfishness, but because I desperately needed him and the help only he could offer. I had a void in my life only he could fill; but at the time I didn't realize that I wanted his *help,* not him. It turned out he *was* the help!

Earl Palmer, a Presbyterian pastor, said that a person who is converted because of fear grows to hate that conversion all his or her life. But a person who is converted out of thirst or need (as I was) grows to love his or her conversion.

Jesus told the woman at the well that if she would drink the water he was offering her, she would thirst no more. And I might add that any other kind of water would never again taste the same. Once we have tasted the water Christ has to offer, no other will fulfill us. We may turn our back on him for a season. Then we either return or remain miserable.

So I can't say my motives in following Christ are entirely pure, but I don't think that makes any difference to him. I believe he accepts me as I am. And I claim the promise of Philippians 1:6 (KJV): "He which hath begun a good work in you will perform it until the day of Jesus Christ."

8

The Right of Destination

When I saw the phrase "the right of destination," it appealed to me greatly. Author Kathryn Lindskoog coined it in *The Lion of Judah in Never-Never Land.*[3] She was referring to one of C. S. Lewis' basic beliefs, namely that we are all children of a King and have a right, as such, to go on a journey to and with him. Eternal life with this King is our destination, our life journey.

In this same regard, consider the first few sentences of George McDonald's fairy tale *The Princess and the Goblin:*[4]

"There was once a little princess who—"
"But, Mr. Author, why do you always write about princesses?"
"Because every little girl is a princess."
"You will make them vain if you tell them that."
"Not if they understand what I mean."
"Then what do you mean?"
"What do you mean by a princess?"
"The daughter of a king."
"Very well, then every little girl is a princess. . . ."

This is also C. S. Lewis' concept of humanity. We are all princes and princesses, the sons and daughters of a King. Although our ultimate destination may be the same, the journey is so different for each of us. Some of us are burdened with almost unbearable cares and sorrows, while others breeze through life. Some of us fulfill most of our potential, while others waste it and fall short of the mark any loving king would will for his princes and princesses.

Lewis was especially cognizant of our obligation to help one another fulfill that potential. In his book *The Weight of Glory*,[5] he spoke of the "glory" of one's neighbor; the "weight" was our call to help the neighbor reach that glory. Even the dullest and most uninteresting person may someday become a person we will greatly admire, "or else a horror and a corruption such as is seen only in a nightmare." Lewis concludes: "All day long we are, in some degree, helping each other to one or the other of these destinations."

Lewis designed his books to help people toward what he considers the right of destination. So it then becomes a sort of play on words. The right of destination is the right to seek the right destination.

As children of God the King, all of us have a tremendous birthright. We have a right to a destiny that can be ours as we seek the destination. We have unlimited, untapped potential, a glory that is unfathomable. We also carry a great weight, a burden to help our neighbor not to become a "horror and corruption such as is seen only in a nightmare," but instead a glorious creature greatly to be admired and appreciated, a prince or princess in all the glorious sense those terms connote.

Yes, we are all sons and daughters of our King. We are all princes and princesses. Some of us may feel like the frog who was enchanted and changed from a prince into that ugly creature. But you'll remember that in the fairy tale the kiss of the lovely princess restored him to his rightful position and form. There are many ways to kiss a frog, but I think the best way is to say, "I love you. I care." When we do that, we help each other become the persons we are intended to be: the children of the King of kings—our rightful destiny!

9

I'll Never Walk Alone

Rodgers and Hammerstein wrote "You'll Never Walk Alone," that hauntingly beautiful song from the musical *Carousel*. None of us wants to be alone, whether we're 16 or 76. We hear most about the problems of loneliness in the aged—those alone, sometimes in nursing homes, with no one to love or care for them. But we don't have to be elderly to be lonely. I suspect some of the loneliest persons around are teenagers—unsure of themselves, not quite at maturity but expected to act mature, with a lot of raw feelings and emotions all covered up so no one will suspect. It's my guess that teenagers are better at wearing a mask than those in any other age group. The lyrics of another beautiful song could apply to them: "laughing on the outside, crying on the inside." Have you ever done that—tried to put on a brave smile and say, "I'm fine, thank you," when your heart was breaking? I know I have.

The sad thing is we need never be lonely, even when we are alone. That applies whether we live in a nursing home with no family to visit us on Christmas Day, or we ache because no one asked us to the senior prom and we couldn't take the risk and go alone.

There is One who has said to us, "I will never leave you or forsake you. I will be with you, even until the end of time." Countless millions can testify to how true those words are. That doesn't mean we'll never be physically alone, but that is different from being lonely. That doesn't mean we'll never hurt again, but it does mean someone will be there to comfort us.

I once heard a respected pastor say, "One of the quickest ways to become bored with your Christian life is to live it alone." I'm sure he's right. The Christian life isn't meant to be lived alone. It is meant to be lived in Christian fellowship, sharing our thoughts and our innermost feelings with those with whom we have a common bond of love and unity—the tie of a shared love for Jesus Christ. When we have that kind of fellowship, we are never alone. It brings excitement and fulfillment. It prevents those feelings of loneliness and despair, and is a marvelous antidote for boredom.

10

God Will Keep Me

All my life I have struggled with temptation. I have tried very hard to overcome this by willpower, by making promises to God and some to myself; but I couldn't resist. I didn't have the strength. Circumstances and conditions sometimes force us into a position where vows are just about impossible to keep. But I've discovered that God keeps bringing me back, time and time again when I've failed. And I've failed many times.

I used to wonder what would have happened if the Prodigal Son had left home again after he had been welcomed back and forgiven by his father. I think I have the answer. I think the power of his father's love would have kept bringing him back no matter how many times he left home. God is even more faithful.

Knowing that God will keep me is a great liberation. It makes the struggle easier. I know God will win out in the end and will never let me go.

God came into my life and stayed. No matter how many times I've turned in the opposite direction, God has always corrected my course. I'm convinced he will do that as long as I live.

Jude 24 tells us that Christ is able to keep us from stumbling and will present us to God blameless and with great joy. Believe it! Also believe Philippians 1:6 (NRSV): "The one who began a good work among you will bring it to completion by the day of Christ Jesus."

11

What Price Beauty?

On a tour of the homes of famous stars near Hollywood, my driver pointed out the magnificent mansion of a famous beauty and star of yesteryear. In her advanced age she was so vain she didn't go out of her house for eight years because she didn't want people to see her as an old person.

I was reminded of Cole Porter who inherited millions from his wealthy family in Peru, Indiana. He then went on to win fame and fortune on his own as one of the most popular songwriters of all time. Who can fail to get a lift out of "Wunderbar" from the 1948 musical *Kiss Me Kate* or be moved by his lilting songs from the 1930s—"Just One of Those Things," "Begin the Beguine," or "Night and Day"?

According to a story I heard, in the latter years of his life Porter was so terrified of death that he rarely went out of his New York penthouse apartment. The story can't be entirely accurate because when I checked an encyclopedia, I found he died in Santa Monica, California, not in New York. Maybe the other story is suspect too. Maybe that famous movie star wasn't vain and afraid of growing old. Whether or not these particular stories are true, we all know individuals like that—so shrivelled up and vain all they want to do is withdraw from life and await death. They await it, not joyfully, but with terror.

Compare this outlook with that of Corrie Ten Boom. After her book *The Hiding Place* was published, and the movie based on the book had been shown across the country, she became famous. Corrie never had the looks to make her a glamorous movie star. While the Hollywood beauty was the rage of two continents, Corrie was fixing watches in her father's shop in Holland and then going through torture in a concentration camp during World War II at the hands of the Germans for befriending Jews, even though she was not one herself.

In later life, who had the beauty? Corrie had an inner beauty and glow. While the glamour queen of years gone by exiled herself to her own home, Corrie, at the same age, was tramping all over the world bringing hope and encouragement to countless millions and undoubtedly experiencing great joy herself.

What enabled Corrie to be an inspiration to millions and to travel worldwide with her message of hope while awaiting her ultimate demise with peace and anticipation? The answer is her personal relationship with Jesus Christ. She knew him, not just as some legendary figure in a history book or even the Bible, but as a real person with whom she had day-to-day, hour-to-hour contact and from whom she received strength and sustenance to go on.

That same personal relationship with Jesus Christ can help all of us overcome the fear of death and keep us from letting a few wrinkles on our faces mar our unique beauty.

12

Ministry—Two Sides of the Coin

I once read *Call to Commitment*,[6] an extremely interesting book by Elizabeth O'Connor, in which she said:

> The fact is that all our lives we will be shifting back and forth between the role of physician and patient, of shepherd and sheep, of parent and child. If ever we arrive at the place where we do not need the ministry of another, we will have arrived at the place of not needing God.

That thought has returned to my mind with new force. To be honest, I once felt I had reached such spiritual heights I could henceforth always be the minister, and would never again need to be ministered to—at least in the way I had needed it in the past. At the time in my life when I was completely broken, I had no strength, spiritual or otherwise. I could never have made it without the deep and abiding love of Jesus Christ as expressed through some beautiful Christian brothers and sisters who were committed to him and, because of that, to me. At that stage of my life I was in no condition to minister to anybody, least of all myself. All I could do was take, not give.

At that time some well-intentioned, but ill-advised, Christians told me the way out was to do something for others. What they didn't understand was a person in that shape *can't* do for others. In the first place, he or she has nothing to give. In the second place, such a person is too depressed to function. Some of Jesus' followers knew this sound psychological principle so many of us tend to forget today. Even after Christ's resurrection victory, Peter was still depressed, very likely because he knew full well his own failure. He knew he had denied (not once, but three times) the Lord whom he had boasted so proudly he would *never* forsake. Put yourself in Peter's shoes. How would you feel if you had denied the Lord three times? Would even the news of Christ's resurrection have cheered you up? Likely not. You would have dreaded facing him, feeling in the depths of your being the duplicity and cowardice you had seen manifested in yourself.

Peter's friends knew this. And did they tell him, "Cheer up, Peter, it isn't so bad. Remember, Jesus gave us the keys of the kingdom. Let's get on with our task of being his instruments to bring salvation to the world"?

No, they knew better. They didn't have a Ph.D. in psychology, but they knew human nature well enough to realize anybody as low as Peter couldn't begin to help anyone. So what did they do? They simply hung in there with him. They just went fishing with him—no lecture, no challenge, no chastisement, just loyal friendship.

At the time in my life when I was the person in need, that was all I *could* be. But as I gradually regained strength (in fact, got *new* strength I'd never had) through the ministry of Christ and Christian friends, I began to feel like reaching out to minister to others and was able to do so. Because of all that had been done for me, I wanted to, as the song goes, "pass it on." Eventually I came to be involved in more ministering situations than in situations where I was ministered to. It almost became a matter of pride with me. Not because I thought I was such a great minister; rather, I thought I had gained sufficient strength so that I'd never again need to call out to others for help. I knew I'd always be calling out to Christ.

Rather than talk in vague generalities, let me be specific. I once kept in my address book a list of prayer groups in cities to which I frequently travelled. It was my thought that I might be in one of those cities some day and need prayer. Several years had gone by, however, since I had made the entries, and it was time to get a new address book. Out of laziness, as well as pride, when I came to enter all those telephone numbers in the new book, I thought to myself, Oh, what the heck! I'll never need those numbers. I'll never be in the shape again where I'll need to call anybody and ask for prayer, or to have to go to a strange prayer meeting in a city away from home.

Just a few days later, after I'd experienced a couple of disappointments, I wished I had those numbers because I needed some help. I needed to be ministered to. Fortunately the Lord provided, and I found the fellowship and prayer support I needed through some new friends in a strange city.

Out of that experience I learned a lesson. I'll *always* be in need of help and prayer support from others. No matter how far I may go on my spiritual journey, there will be times when I'll need to be ministered to, as well as the more fulfilling times when I can do the ministering.

The Lord didn't keep me in that position long. The point was made, and I was brought back up out of the valley. But I guess we all need those valley experiences from time to time, as depressing as they may be, to keep us humble and mindful of the fact that our strength comes from the Lord and is frequently extended to us through the love, support, and prayer of others.

I think God likes to be asked to help. In C. S. Lewis' tale *The Magician's Nephew*,[7] a flying horse (Fledge), a girl (Polly), and a boy (Digory) are talking about Aslan, the great Lion in the land of Narnia. The dialogue goes like this:

> "Well I *do* think someone might have arranged about our meals," said Digory.
> "I'm sure Aslan would have, if you'd asked Him," said Fledge.
> "Wouldn't He know without being asked?" said Polly.
> "I've no doubt He would," said the Horse. "But I've a sort of an idea He likes to be asked."

I think the Horse is right. I think Christ does like to

be asked. And I think sometimes he may even want us to be in the position of having to ask others to ask him for us. That's a humbling experience! Next time I won't throw away those telephone numbers.

13

Kindness

Someone once asked me what I thought was the most desirable trait in a wife. I answered, "Kindness—someone who is kind."

I once saw the play *The Elephant Man*. It's about a grotesque and monstrously deformed man who lived in London in the late 1800s. He was abandoned by his mother because she couldn't bear to look at him. His early life was in a workhouse where he was continually beaten. Then a schemer saw his potential as a sideshow freak and capitalized on the theory that people would pay to see him because it would make them feel so much better about themselves.

Abandoned by his "patron" when he was no longer drawing crowds, this pathetic young man became the ward of a London hospital for his last four years of life. A doctor helped him, but the Elephant Man still felt rejection and hurt.

In the play he talks to the doctor about those who, although they didn't hurt him physically, were insensitive to his deepest needs. He speaks the most poignant line in the play: "Your mercy is so cruel. What do you have for justice?"

Genuine mercy is *not* cruel. Kindness and mercy and justice are inseparable—and very much in our lives—if we are true followers of Jesus Christ. Some of his most sensitive teaching comes in the Beatitudes where we are told to be merciful.

Webster's dictionary uses the word *compassion* in defining *mercy. Compassion* is defined as "sympathetic consciousness of others' distress together with a desire to alleviate it."

Kindness is defined by these words: "affectionate, loving, sympathetic, forebearing, friendly, gentle, helpful, and considerate."

Justice is defined with the words "fair, to show appreciation for."

Yet even in so-called Christian homes and in relationships between Christians, these qualities of mercy, kindness, and justice are sometimes sorely lacking. Husbands and wives are not kind and merciful to each other; the justice they mete out is one-sided and shows no appreciation for the other person. Demanding parents do not take into consideration the thoughts, feelings, and needs of their children.

I know of one wife who learned of a weakness in her husband and admittedly "tried to hurt him where he was the most vulnerable." There is no mercy in such actions—no kindness, no justice. That is cruelty at its worst. It is just as cruel as what was done to the Elephant Man. Emotional beatings can be just as severe as physical ones—sometimes more so.

Webster defines *cruelty* as "disposed to inflict pain; causing injury, grief or pain unrelieved by leniency." Let's examine our hearts and our actions. Are we inflicting pain, hurt, and grief on others? Or are we ministering with mercy, kindness, and justice? Are we treating those around us like "elephant men" because of some grotesqueness or flaw we see in them?

The most moving moment in the play comes when a beautiful lady reaches out to touch the hideous mass of flesh that was the Elephant Man. It is reminiscent of Jesus' reaching out and touching the leper. Do we reach out in love to those around us, or can the charge be leveled at us: "Your mercy is so cruel. What do you have for justice?"

14

Forgiveness

Anger and unforgiveness are blood relatives. Both can make our blood boil. It's very difficult to forgive anybody we're angry with. And if we don't forgive, we're likely to stay angry. It's a vicious circle. How do we break it? Do we stop being angry so we can forgive, or do we forgive so we can stop being angry? That's a tough one. If I had to make a choice, I would say it is the latter. If we can somehow forgive the other person, we can stop being angry at her or him. And I think I have a handle on how we can do that.

But first, let's look at forgiveness itself. What is forgiveness? Suppose we say (or imply) to the other person, "If you'll admit you were wrong, if you'll say you're sorry, if you'll confirm I was right and you were wrong, I'll forgive you." Is that forgiveness? Technically perhaps, but conditional forgiveness really isn't forgiveness at all. I don't think it's the type of forgiveness Christ was talking about when he told Peter he must forgive "seventy times seven."

There wasn't any condition to Jesus' prayer "Father,

forgive them, for they know not what they do." He didn't preface that request with, "If you'll take these nails out of my hands and take me down off this cross and admit you were bad boys in hanging me up here and say you're sorry, I'll ask God to forgive you, and I'll forgive you too." Instead Jesus said, in effect, "Even though you aren't even sorry, I'm still going to ask God to forgive you. I forgive you too because you don't even realize what you are doing."

What do you think Jesus would say to those who did realize what they were doing, who knew in their hearts that they were nailing the Son of God to the cross? Sin, Jesus said, is that "light has come into the world, and people loved darkness rather than light" (John 3:19 NRSV).

I think it's relatively easy to forgive the person who comes to us and says he or she is sorry and wants another chance. Some of us, though, won't even go that far. We say, "No, you've blown it. I'm not going to give you any more chances."

When I've known someone like that, I've had trouble forgiving him or her for being unforgiving. That's really a vicious circle! But I still say even unforgiveness by the other person is no reason for our not granting forgiveness, even if the person doesn't realize she or he needs it and isn't asking for it. If we want to be authentic, genuine Christians and not hypocrites or poor witnesses for the Lord of love and forgiveness, we must forgive regardless.

I think such forgiveness is an impossible goal for a

human being who is trying to do it on his or her own. Certain things just can't be forgiven by willpower. The hurts run too deep. The bitterness is too cancerous. To forgive in such cases goes against the grain of human nature, emotions, and feelings. We have a tendency to insist we have the last word and to want to be proven right, if not in the eyes of the world, then at least in our own eyes. Whether it's a lack of emotional maturity or just plain cussedness, we want the one who wronged us to be shown for the cur he is, the insensitive person she is underneath. We want the world to know what we know about them.

Maybe this isn't true of all of us. I hope it isn't. But let's be honest. I don't think, though, we need to feel guilty because of these feelings. They're honest feelings because we *have* them. That doesn't make them right or wrong. There is no moral implication to them. If they are genuine and real, and honestly ours, let's face up to them and admit them. When we get them out on the table and take a good, healthy look at them, we can make a rational, responsible decision about what to do with them.

We can make the choice to nurse feelings of resentment and unforgiveness and thereby nurture them, cling to them with all our being, make them gods, all in order to prove the other person wrong. We can also try to forgive by sheer willpower. I think that's an impossible task.

Our last alternative, and I think our best one, is to ask for help. To say something like, "Lord, you know my feelings of unforgiveness. You know that I feel I have been wronged. I know I can nurse that feeling till hell freezes over, but I don't really want to do that. If I do that and at the same time proclaim I'm a Christian, I'm being a hypocrite, and that isn't what you want me to do. It isn't what you did. There's no question that the Bible says to forgive, regardless. So in the words of Catherine Marshall, please treat the act of my will as the act of the real me, even though my emotions protest vehemently.[8] My emotions are crying out that I can't forgive, I *won't* forgive until he admits he's wrong. But the real me is saying to you that I *do* forgive. So please accept that as the real me. Please be the active agent of forgiveness. I can't handle it. I give it to you. Do what you have to do. Paraphrasing the man who said, 'I believe. Help my unbelief,' I say to you, 'I forgive. Help my unforgiveness.'"

I think that's all we can do—there's no other choice. I'm utterly convinced God respects and demands total honesty. No phony baloney business with God! No rationalization. No pious phrases covering a rebellious heart. No hypocrisy. Remember Jesus' story about the two men who prayed in the temple? One said, "Thank God I'm better than other men. Thank God I'm not a sinner." The other prayed, "Forgive me, a miserable sinner." And he was the one who found acceptance by God.

15

The Great Liberator

In his book *Guilt and Grace,*[9] Paul Tournier says: "Living means choosing, and choosing means running the risk of making mistakes, and accepting the risk of being guilty of making mistakes." When we fail and make mistakes, we have a tendency to feel guilty about it. This fear of making mistakes, this great reluctance to feel guilty paralyzes us.

What is this fear of failure anyway? Could it be a dislike for the uncomfortable and depressing feeling guilt fosters in our unconscious mind when we fail, a sort of self-blame? If we dislike that feeling so much, we will avoid it at all costs, even if the avoidance paralyzes us. But if we know we are able to deal with the guilt, should it come, then won't we be much more likely to act?

It seems to me that willingness to accept mistakes if they come is a great liberating force. How freeing to be able to say, "So what if I fail!" Or even more liberating, "So what if I fail, there's someone (Christ) who will pick me up if I do!"

I've heard it said and preached that if we can receive

forgiveness for our sins against God, we will immediately experience a release and a sense of peace. I've seen that philosophy in print so many times—just accept God's forgiveness for those sins. But it isn't that simple. Sometimes we haven't forgiven ourselves for our sins against ourselves.

At one stage in my life, I could easily accept forgiveness for what I had done against God, but I was still depressed. In fact, I really wasn't concerned about what I'd done against God. I wasn't aware of my wrong attitudes. What concerned me, what depressed me was what I had done to myself. I couldn't forgive myself, and that caused the depression.

It took me a long time to work through all that, with Christ's help—to be able to love, forgive, and accept myself. When I could finally do that, the depression vanished. And the remarkable thing was that, in the wake of healthy forgiveness of myself and the departure of depression, I could then clearly see my sin against God. I couldn't see it while I was so wrapped up in self-hate.

Tournier also speaks to this point in *Guilt and Grace:*[10]

> To offer grace only is to cut off half the Gospel. Grace is for the woman [caught in adultery] trembling at her guilt. But her accusers will be able to find grace only by rediscovering for themselves the shudder of guilt. On the other hand, to present only the sternness of God also cuts off half the Gospel. Jesus does not awaken guilt in order to

condemn, but to save, for grace is given to him who humbles himself, and becomes aware of his guilt.

When we finally see our guilt, God takes it away. But when we don't see it, when it is repressed or suppressed, God brings it to the surface and then blots it out again with free grace. That grace is the great liberator that allows us to have the healthy and freeing attitude of "So what if I fail, there's someone who will pick me up if I do." When we see that Romans 8:28 (KJV) is true—"All things work together for good to them that love God"— we are free, liberated from the paralyzing fear of making mistakes. We have made mistakes and have learned that Christ can work them into a pattern for good.

That knowledge can only come through experience. We first have to fail, to live through the awful agony of seeing our human weakness and sin. Then as we see our lives being transformed by the grace of God, we can experience true liberation.

16

Judging

Those of us who have felt ourselves judged (is there anyone who hasn't?) know the devastating result the judgments of others (fair or unfair, warranted or unwarranted) can bring. If the judgment is accepted into our psyche, the result can be feelings of guilt and inferiority that can destroy the human spirit.

I mentioned in the last chapter Paul Tournier's magnificent treatise on guilt and guilt feelings. In *Guilt and Grace*[11] he not only makes a plea for the cessation of harsh and cruel judgments that bind and entrap us, but also analyzes different kinds or qualities of guilt. He talks about the "guilt of doing" and the "guilt of being." The guilt of doing is the remorse we feel for a particular action or inaction, some failure in life that brings to light a weakness inherent in our nature. When we fail in some way, the vultures are so prone to jump in and shout "guilty as charged."

If blaming and judgment are the great dividers (and they unquestionably are), then what is the healing agent that can reconcile people and bring them back together?

Christ himself, of course, is the great reconciler, as St. Paul wrote in 2 Corinthians 5:18, 19 and Ephesians 2:15, 16. But what means can accomplish this? I believe it is the Holy Spirit who reveals to us our weakness and inadequacies. When we are able to face up to and accept responsibility for those weaknesses, we are less apt to blame and criticize other people (see Ephesians 4:15, 16, 25, 30-32). When we become aware of the piece of wood in our own eye, we are less apt to focus on and complain bitterly about the splinter in our neighbor's eye (Matthew 7:4, 5).

Speaking to this point, Tournier says in *Guilt and Grace:*[12]

> What can bring [men] together is the consciousness of their common misery. . . . This [human condition] can bring them together, reconcile them, unite them in a common humbling and a common liberation . . . a common awareness of human weakness . . . brings men together in a common repentance.

Until we have seen our own human condition in the light and brilliance of God's love and grace, until we can face up to our own inadequacies, failings, and weaknesses (often shown to us in failure and the pain of the accompanying guilt feelings), we will continue to judge and blame others. We need to realize we don't have all the answers either. And yet, while we continue to make mistakes, God continues to love us. When we feel God's love and understanding at the point of our own failure, we can love not only ourselves, but others who also fail.

17

A Change in Attitude

I suppose most of us know at least a few Christians who are very judgmental and abrasive and unloving. Hollywood has done a good job of caricaturing these types. *Inherit the Wind,* the motion picture with Spencer Tracy and Frederic March, is a perfect example. March portrayed William Jennings Bryan, who assisted the prosecution in the now famous Scopes Monkey Trial, in which a teacher was prosecuted for teaching evolution. What Bryan was really like, I don't know. I'd hate to think he was as narrow and unloving as March portrayed him.

But to me, the arch-villain of the piece wasn't Bryan, but a minister who was the father of the girl young Scopes, the teacher, was dating. He ranted and raved and condemned the girl to hell for even dating this young man who was advocating the possibility of a theory alien to his own.

That attitude makes me think of Jesus' admonition not to throw the first stone (John 8:7). We are so quick to judge and condemn others, when it's quite possible that if we were in their shoes, we would act no differently. I know of a Christian woman, a widow, who dated a married man. I'm sure many Christians would immediately jump up and say, "How terrible," "How awful," and (in effect) stone her.

While I'm not condoning what she did, I can *understand.* I know something of her background and some extremely tough times she had. I understand her loneliness, for I have had loneliness in my own life and know how devastating it can be. I think perhaps the first women to condemn her might be those who have a husband coming home to them every night, and the first men to condemn her could be those with a loving wife and children. How easy to condemn when things are going well for us. How easy to cast stones when we're in the catbird seat and all our emotional needs are being met.

Those who are lonely can, I believe, better understand how a lonely widow, even a Christian one, might be tempted to seek or accept companionship to help fill the long, empty hours—even if that companionship was wrong in some ways or might not be according to the rules prescribed by society or the church. I can understand how a lonely man or woman could be tempted in sexual areas outside the bonds of matrimony. I don't want to cast stones at homosexuals, who apparently cannot relate in some ways to the opposite sex, yet still have emotional and sexual drives like any other human being.

Again, I'm most certainly *not* saying, "Let the bars down. Lower the claims of Christ to ease the human conscience." I think far too many Christians have done that.

No, we should not lower the claims. We should not paint over what is wrong or wink at it. What matters is the *attitude* with which we speak out and challenge.

One of the best examples of love in the Bible is King David's friend Nathan coming to him and telling him he had been wrong in taking another man's wife and then having her husband killed. Nathan loved David so much he risked his own neck to challenge his king, David, because it was in David's best interest. That is real, unselfish love.

I suspect far too many parents today are afraid of their own children. They are afraid to speak words of admonition or correction and thereby incur the children's wrath or lose their love. To me that is weakness. Strength is taking a stand in love. But when we do take those stands, we need to search our own hearts first, put ourselves in their shoes, honestly think through how we would react if we were they.

It's so easy to say, "Oh, I would react differently." But would we? How do we know unless we've been there ourselves? And even if we have been there, even if we have been able to master temptation to which others have succumbed, we must never be arrogant about it. There is nothing that destroys a Christian's witness faster than spiritual pride, an "I'm better than you are" attitude. And I suspect nothing is as unbecoming in the eyes of our Lord. Isn't that what Jesus reacted against while on this earth—the self-righteousness of the Pharisees?

18

We Should Be Ashamed

One of the sorriest aspects of Christianity, and certainly its poorest witness, is Christians fighting among themselves. If you've been a Christian very long, you've possibly seen it in your own church. You've undoubtedly read about it in the papers. One of the major denominations is split right down the middle over a fundamental versus a perhaps slightly more flexible interpretation of the Bible. Several years ago the charismatic community suffered through some real hostility over who was right and who was wrong about something called "shepherding," a concept where one person as a shepherd takes much direct control over another person's life. Quite a few churches were split when some of the members, or even the pastor, suddenly began speaking in tongues. The ones who didn't speak (or pray) in tongues felt that the ones who did were fanatics or on the lunatic fringe. Some of those who spoke in tongues went around saying that the ones who didn't weren't "saved." I remember speaking to a zealous man about one of the best-known ministers in the United States, and he said, "Why, he isn't even saved."

No wonder we Christians at times fail to show the world outside of Christ anything they want to have in their own lives. They see us fightin' and feudin' and say to themselves, "No, thank you. We want none of that."

A dear friend of mine attended college in the East. He had been a Christian since he was eleven, and he really knows and loves the Lord. While at college, he wrote his father about how some of the Christians in his college were turning off the non-Christians. Speaking of some of his non-Christian classmates, he said:

> They are open to friendship. That may seem very simple, but think about it. A kid down the hall wants to be respected. He is a very respectable guy. He knows that I respect him and what he believes. But he is upset with the way Christians refuse to acknowledge another individual's opinion and point of view. In talking with me he revealed just why the Christians on campus are so rejected. They are on a crusade. Their motives are so Christian they aren't even very friendly anymore. Is that being Christian? Isn't our first motive love? Although Christians claim humility, most non-Christians don't always see it because, while it is humility before God, to men it is proud arrogance. Other men want Christians to respect them as people with a point of view. To me the only way to sincerely express yourself to people is to show them that, first of all, you care about

them as people, regardless of whether they become Christians, and second you want to add to their lives and give them some insight into finding real joy.

How much insight this young man had gained at a very early age! I'd like to be able to tell him I have measured up to his ideal at every turn. I haven't.

Ironically I have more tolerance for non-Christians than I do for many Christians. I can relate better to where non-Christians are because I was one myself for a long time. I empathize with them, even sympathize with them, and don't condemn them. But the ones I have trouble with are the Christians who don't agree with me, who preach the Gospel in a way I don't think it should be preached, who don't love people the way I think they should be loved. I'm afraid that's also a poor example to the non-Christian world.

What kind of example have Christians been, down through the ages? They put others to death in the Inquisition for heresies that were only heresies by their standards. They tried to torture and browbeat Native Americans into worshipping a God who could scarcely seem a God of love and mercy, judging by those who claimed to be his followers. What about the newspaper headlines of Christians fighting a "Holy War," and two opposing so-called Christian forces in Ireland, bombing and terrorizing innocent women and children?

I say we should be ashamed. We evidence little in our

own lives as faithful followers of the Christ who commands us to love one another. As 1 John 4:20 (NRSV) puts it: "Those who say, 'I love God,' and hate their brothers or sisters, are liars; for those who do not love a brother or sister whom they have seen, cannot love God whom they have not seen."

19

The Search for Something Else

"The Search for Something Else" was a documentary on television. Another title could have been "The Consciousness Movement" or "The New Consciousness"— terms frequently used on the program.

Millions of our citizens are on the "search for something else," for a power inside themselves that will give meaning to life. One successful businessman interviewed on the program said that, although he had achieved all the material rewards, he still felt empty and went searching for something to fill the vacuum. What he found was a guru and a form of Eastern religion, which he now says is the answer. Others have found their "answer" in TM, est, Hare Krishna, or simply contemplating their navel.

How insidious these consciousness movements are. How deceptive! They suck in hungry people and give them a counterfeit answer, one that eventually may lead them to great sorrow. Many are selling their birthright for a mess of pottage.

A proponent of one of the consciousness movements said it was a "new dimension—inward to the self." He went on to say, "That which you call God, the universe, the self are basically the same."

We Christians believe God is in us through the Holy Spirit, but that doesn't begin to make us God. To say we and God are "basically the same" is a gross misconception of our Christian faith. I am amazed more Christian ministers don't speak out strongly against these perversions and amazed even a few have found a basic accommodation between these views and Christianity.

The movement, though, does point out vividly the vacuum in the human heart and soul, the longing to be fulfilled that is in all of us. We were made that way. As Pascal so aptly told us, there is a God-shaped vacuum in the human heart. I'm convinced our God made us that way, knowing only fellowship with the Divine could fill that vacuum to overflowing.

20

Legalism or Lovism

Legalism is a term most Christians know. It refers to a harsh set of "thou shalt nots" plucked from the Bible. In some cases its adherents even "proof-text," picking isolated verses out of the Bible to prove a point. Sometimes the verses are taken out of context and their meaning distorted to something entirely different from what the true meaning is in the context and flow of the other surrounding verses.

Another failing of many Christians is to judge those who have different views. We often seem to be harder on our brothers and sisters in Christ than we are on those who don't believe at all.

I struggle with the legalists because many of them show little love, compassion, or mercy. To them, living is a set of rules; and if others don't keep the rules as interpreted by them, then the non-conformists aren't even "saved." I think that contradicts the Bible. I don't see how anyone can read the Bible and fail to sense its compelling message of love, mercy, forgiveness, and reconciliation.

Far too often Christians have forsaken their biblical heritage and mandate. God's Word is not being preached and taught from many of the pulpits of our land. Yet the law without the tempering love and gentleness of the Holy Spirit is deadly. As 2 Corinthians 3:6 (NRSV) puts it, "The letter kills, but the Spirit gives life." Similarly, being guided only by the Holy Spirit without the guidance of the Word can so easily lead to emotionalism.

I think what we need is less legalism and more of what I like to call *lovism.* Lovism is the core message of the Bible. It is the gospel of Jesus Christ come to life. It is expressed through caring and forgiveness—reaching out in love, compassion, and affirmation. It is a ministry of reconciliation—reconciling ourselves not only to God but also to one another. It is Christ saying to the woman caught in adultery: "Neither do I condemn thee; go, and sin no more" (John 8:11 KJV).

I think lovism means "I may not agree with you, but if I can learn about what has contributed to who you are and why you acted as you did, then it will be so much easier for me to understand you and forgive you for hurting me."

Lovism is Christ telling Peter he must forgive, not just seven times but "seventy times seven." Lovism is Mother Teresa in Calcutta devoting her life to the poor and dying. Lovism is opening up our home to someone crushed, down and out, without employment or hope, and on the verge of suicide, and saying in words and actions, "I care." It is a wife saying to her husband who has apologized and asked for forgiveness, "Of course I forgive you. I will do my best to cherish and comfort you as I promised God I would." It is a husband saying to his wife, "I'm sorry if I have hurt you. I want to understand your emotional needs and be used by God to help meet them."

It amazes me that so many of us can read about Jesus' life—what he did, what he taught, what he lived out by example—and not get the big picture. We are here to love and follow him, and love and care for our brothers and sisters—to be God's reconciling agents in the world.

21

What Is Power?

Earl Palmer, a Presbyterian pastor, once said in a sermon, "New Testament power is not power over people so I can manipulate them. Rather, it is my assurance that God has the power. It is my assurance that, no matter how bad a situation gets, Jesus Christ has the power to help." Palmer expresses that same thought somewhat differently in his book, *Salvation by Surprise*:[13] "The secret to the strength of the Christian is that Jesus Christ is Lord."

I've seen that power at work in my own life. When Jesus Christ came into my life, he slowly but surely picked up the pieces and put them back together in a much better way than ever before. His mark is on a life that had failed on its own power.

Palmer also said, in reference to power, "When people try to become saviors, it is dangerous. Jesus Christ is the Savior. All we're to do is be his witnesses. That's our commission."

I'm sure we all have seen dozens of well-meaning Christians who think they have the power to "save" us.

They have all the answers, and if we don't do it their way, then we're going the wrong way on a one-way street.

It's unfortunate, but so many of these well-intentioned people succeed in doing the exact opposite of what they intend to do. They turn people away from "religion" and Jesus Christ. If these Christians only knew that the best way to reach others is to love them, to hang in there with them when the going gets rough, and to tell them about the only One who really can help—the One who loves unconditionally.

22

A Common Bond

In college days I belonged to a fraternity, a group with a very close bond. We even had a secret handshake and a way to end our letters that would identify us as brothers. That bond meant a lot to us. It brought us close together, not only to the brothers in our own chapter, but also to the brothers in chapters across the country. Whenever we met a brother from another college, we immediately had something in common, something that drew us together.

If being members of the same fraternity creates a bond, think about how much more of a bond Christians share. The central core of the college fraternity is the fellowship and the tradition. Christianity has that going for it too, but it has so much more. It has—or should have—at its core the Person of Christ. Jesus is our rallying point, our cause, something we can *really* get excited about—that is, if we know him personally.

It's difficult to get excited about an historic figure, if that's all Jesus is to us. But if he's our best friend and our

Lord, someone who is with us all the time, someone we can talk to—and at times even listen to—then we have an excitement we want to share with others who feel the same way we do.

I was a loyal fraternity man in college and had a lot of pride in our group, but it was nothing to compare with the joy, excitement, and fulfillment I find in Christianity. When I meet another brother or sister in Christ, someone who understands what a personal relationship with him is all about, I get excited. We usually enjoy a beautiful time of sharing and fellowship.

Sometimes Christians are misunderstood when they ask the question, "Are you a Christian?" Sometimes, I'll admit, it is said in a judgmental way, as much as to say, "Well, if you aren't a Christian, I don't want anything to do with you." But I don't think that was the way it was meant back in the church of the first century, and I hope it isn't usually meant that way today. I think back then it was said in wonderment—"Is he one of us?" "Is she our sister?" "Has he found the same meaning in life we have?" "Does she know Christ too?" Christianity is not exclusive like a fraternity—it's open to everyone.

Early Christians signed their letters with an indication they were a "Christ one" or a "Christian." Look at all of Paul's Epistles. He signed those letters to Christians to indicate their family relationship. I have some dear Christian brothers now who never fail to sign their letters to me with "In Christ," "In his love," "Yours in Christ," or "Your Brother." I usually do the same when I'm writing someone with whom I share the common bond of Christ.

It's a great bond. It means so very much to me. So do my brothers and sisters in that bond.

23

Sensitivity

Sensitivity is a two-pronged trait. It can be a beautiful and most desirable trait, or it can be one we're better off not having. Webster defines *sensitive* as "very keenly susceptible to stimuli." The key is "susceptible." In what *ways* are we susceptible? How does our keen susceptibility affect us? It can affect us in a positive or a negative way. Let's look first at the negative aspects.

Most of us have heard of or know someone who is easily offended by another's remarks or actions. I knew a person who took great offense when her lifelong friends invited another couple to sit in their box at a football game. These friends had also provided 50-yard-line grandstand seats for this sensitive person and her husband, but she refused to speak to them for three years. I'm not sure she ever totally forgave. Her lifelong philosophy was "Keep your eye picked; the world's agin you. You've got to think about yourself because if you don't, nobody else will." I'd say she was sensitive, but not in a healthy sense. Most negative feelings of sensitivity come from a poor self-image. If we truly feel good about ourselves, what others think and say really doesn't matter.

Barry Goldwater's campaign slogan when he ran for President in 1964 was "In your heart you know he's right." Well, if you know in your heart you're okay, then what others say about you isn't so important. It's like the old saying "Sticks and stones may break my bones, but names can never hurt me."

There are degrees of this negative form of sensitivity. One of the extremes is paranoia—when a person feels that others are persecuting him or her. Have you seen the bumper sticker that says "Just because you're not paranoid doesn't mean they're not out to get you"? Those of you who have read Herman Wouk's *The Caine Mutiny* or have seen the movie version with Humphrey Bogart portraying the paranoiac Captain Queeg know a perfect example of a sick man with a persecution complex. Queeg thought the "world," especially the men on his ship, were "agin" him. Yes, he was sensitive, but who wants to be sensitive in that way?

But there's another form of sensitivity that is desirable. We have an example of that in another book—the Bible. The man there who embodies the truly sensitive person in the good sense is Jesus Christ himself. He was a person keenly susceptible to others, always taking time to listen, to hear the other person out, to understand, and to respond. No man of superficial judgments he, no first-century Archie Bunker—an example of a totally insensitive man as portrayed in the 1970s television show "All in the Family."

I've known men and women who had this deep sensitivity to others. They could understand others' innermost feelings, longings, hurts, and joys. They were there when needed, ready and willing to share the tragedies and victories of life with other human beings. And it is usually the case that people who are so sensitive to others in this good sense are people who are not closed themselves. Rather, they are open and willing to tell you about themselves, who they are, where they hurt, where they've failed, and where they hope to gain victories in the future. They accept themselves so totally (the good with the bad) they don't have to put up some kind of front. They feel no need to appear strong when they know and accept weakness and humanity. Their confidence lies not in themselves but in the One who made them and sustains them through all the trials and tribulations of life.

In many ways, they are "wounded healers," to use Henri Nouwen's phrase—people who have been deeply hurt themselves. Because of that hurt, they long to help others achieve the wholeness they have experienced through the aid of the only One who can bring true wholeness and meaning to any human life. Their sensitivity has been acquired in the school of hard knocks. Their teacher has been the One who had perfect sensitivity and promised to give us an Agent (the Holy Spirit) who would indwell us and enable us to be sensitive not only to God, but also to others.

We need to be both sensitive and not sensitive at the same time. We need to open ourselves up in love to others, but close ourselves to selfish thoughts of inadequacy, persecution, and deprivation of our own emotional needs. We must not be either an insensitive Archie Bunker or a sensitive Captain Queeg, but model ourselves after Jesus Christ.

24

We Are All Ministers

One Sunday I heard a visiting pastor from England, Michael Green, say: "The New Testament has no idea of a Christian who isn't a minister."

Richard Halverson, former chaplain of the United States Senate, says that we are *all* called to be ministers and that the distinction between clergy and laity is a false one. *Laity* means "people of God," says Dr. Halverson, and in that respect, the clergy are no different from other persons in their congregation. Clergy and parishioners alike are laity, people of God, even ministers. The clergy have one main function: equipping and teaching their flock to be better ministers. But the plumber or the lawyer is also called by God to be a minister. They also have people to whom they can and need to be ministering.

Henri Nouwen, a sensitive Catholic priest and psychologist, calls us all to be ministers. In an article appearing in *Sojourners* magazine, he said:

> Our real gifts only become known to us when they are recognized and affirmed by those who receive them. . . .

What more beautiful ministry is there than the ministry by which we make others aware of the love, truth and beauty they reveal to us? Ours is a time in which many people doubt their self-worth and are often on the verge of self-condemnation, not seldom leading to suicide. We can indeed save lives by seeing in the eyes of those in need, and hearing in their words, the story which speaks of the gifts they have to share.

How beautiful, then, is the ministry by which we can call forth the hidden gifts of people and celebrate with them the love, truth and beauty they give us. . . . For most of us, the greater part of our lives are spent not on the mountaintop, but in the valley. And in this valley we are called to be ministers.

I have been ministered to by some dear brothers and sisters in the Lord who have seen the good in me (along with the bad). They have nurtured my possibilities through encouragement, love, and affirmation. They have not dwelt on the bad or engaged in destructive criticism. They have loved me not only for who I am, but also for who they knew I *could* be through God's love and the life-transforming power of Jesus Christ.

All these people were laity, people of God. Some were ordained ministers. Some were not ordained. But all were ministers. Michael Green is so right: "The New Testament has no idea of a Christian who isn't a minister."

25

"If God Be for Us"

As the apostle Paul says in Romans 8: "If God be for us, who can be against us?" But do we really believe God is *for* us? Or do we believe that God is some sort of ogre who is out to deny us all joy and prevent our happiness on this earth?

If we think God is an ogre, then Bible commands are odious. But if we truly believe God is for us, then obedience becomes easier. We obey not just because God told us to, but because it will be to our benefit in the long run.

I once attended a class called "The Christian and Emotion," taught by Dr. Arch Hart, a clinical psychologist and professor in a graduate school of psychology. Dr. Hart said, "God always offers us what is good for us. God deals with us on the basis of our good. Unless we go on that basis, the whole issue of Christian ethics becomes confused." Dr. Hart used envy as one specific example. He sees envy as a continuum on a line that begins with a wish or ambition and culminates in murder. Envy is a kissing cousin of and one step behind covetousness, which God expressly forbids.

But why does God list covetousness as one of the prohibitions in the Ten Commandments? Why does Paul say in 1 Corinthians 13 that "love envieth not"? Is coveting a good that an ogre God is denying us? Or does God know that coveting and longing for something that is not ours, and possibly never can be, will only bring us misery and not joy?

Discontent is a symptom of envy. It is also a cancer of the soul. No discontented person is ever truly happy. Happiness is always one day away, one new car away, one better house away, one exchange of a wife or husband away, one bigger paycheck away.

Even the lovely song "Tomorrow" from the 1977 musical *Annie* is slightly misleading. The lyrics tell us that everything is going to be bright tomorrow. While we do need to look forward to tomorrow to be healthy, while we do need to have hope for better tomorrows to spur us on and keep us from lethargically dwelling in a rut, we can't live in tomorrows. We can only live in todays. And if we are discontent today, we will not be happy. That is why a loving God, who knows the emotional sickness that comes from wanting what we cannot have, tells us not to covet or be envious.

Dr. Hart's definition of mental health is "the ability to adopt an attitude of contentment in a situation that cannot be changed. If you can change the situation, do it. If you can't change your situation, change yourself."

The apostle Paul learned to be content through a process. It was a cultivation of right thoughts, a right perspective (God's perspective) on his lot in life, and right priorities. He could see the larger issues, how everything fits together. He was a happy man while chained in prison and as he went to his execution. His oppressor, the emperor Nero, who had an overabundance of the world's goods, was the most unhappy of men. Even from his position of power and wealth, he was still coveting what he did not have.

As Dr. Hart puts it, "What you've got is everything, if you have God." Happiness comes from within, not from our external circumstances. Yet so many people don't believe that. They spend their whole life coveting external things, which never bring the joy of a personal and obedient relationship with Jesus Christ.

So when God says to do or not to do something, we need to realize that God wants what is best for us, what is good for us. Telling us not to covet or envy is only one example. God's wisdom and truth go to the very core of human existence. God does not want to deprive us but wants us to be truly happy and so has given us a guideline for living. Aren't we rather foolish, then, when we strike out on our own, seeking happiness in ways forbidden to us?

From personal experience, I can say that the old hymn chorus, "Trust and obey, for there's no other way," contains great wisdom. No other way, that is, if we want a joyful and meaningful existence.

26

Outward Circumstances

In *Adaptation to Life* by George Vaillant, I have come across many interesting insights. The book reports a study of the reasons a select group of men either failed or succeeded.

Too many of us do not take into account outward circumstances when we judge the success or failure of another human being. Some of us, unfortunately, even take an "I'd *never* do that if I were you" attitude. Dr. Vaillant makes the very wise observation that some break under the outward circumstances, while others, equally vulnerable and prone to failure, never do crack because their outward life has held up. They have never been subject to the vicissitudes and ill fortune that those who failed had to contend with. They would also probably have cracked in different circumstances.

Here is how Vaillant puts it in *Adaptation to Life*:[14]

Indeed the lack of social supports turned out to be as powerful a predictor of which men sought psychotherapy as their actual psychopathology. . . .

The conditions that tend to foster symptoms of psychiatric disability are those that deprive the individual of self-esteem, love, mentors, self-determination, and a stable place within the social system.

According to Vaillant, those who adapted best to life had stable childhoods, stable marriages, church affiliations, athletics for expressing aggression, and political identification with the status quo. The men "who had unhappy childhoods and lacked social supports were far more likely to use neurotic defenses maladaptively and to seek psychotherapy."

Vaillant gives two case histories of men who were equally prone to failure. The differences in the two men were not so much in the dangers against which they had to defend themselves as in the outside help on which they could rely.

Mr. P enjoyed the support of formal religious affiliation, a happy marriage, and competitive sports with good friends. Mr. L had few supports to fall back on. He was supported neither by his marriage nor by church membership. Mr. L was destroyed by his psychological maladaptations. Mr. P won praise.

Here we have two equally vulnerable men, one achieving success, the other blowing it. Inward stability was not the differentiating determinant in this comparison. Outward circumstances were. If Mr. L's marriage were healthy like Mr. P's, or if a supportive church environment had been part of his world, he might also have been a "success."

I don't want to carry this analogy too far. Carried to the extreme it could lead to a pity-poor-me attitude: "I'm not responsible for my actions. My circumstances are." That is definitely unhealthy. Yet there is a balance, a tension here. Circumstances can be a determinant in success or failure.

I have no easy answers, no panacea for those who are unfortunate enough to have some of the major breaks of life go against them. While an unsupportive wife can affect a husband's career or a brutish, unloving husband can lead to a wife's mental breakdown, we are not helpless in a bad situation, not as helpless as Vaillant's study might lead us to believe. Every man or woman *can* have a "support system" that will help him or her to weather the most severe storm, whether it be emotional or caused by outward circumstances. That support is Jesus Christ.

While we'd all like solid marriages and good outward circumstances, we can still be successes in life without them. Just about all my outward support systems have failed me at some time. I did not have a good marriage. My career came apart in midstream. I have been alienated from those I love most. I would undoubtedly have been labeled a "failure" at one point in my life.

Yet life goes on. At a later point in time, I think even discerning psychiatrists might have had to reevaluate their judgment on my life. My life didn't *end* in failure, as it so easily could have. The final chapter is yet to be written. I was given a whole new way of coping with life's difficulties. No longer was I forced to use my own ineffective defense mechanisms. I was able to begin to substitute Christ's wisdom for mine. Abdicating the throne of my life, I asked him to run the show. I wasn't a king sitting on that throne anyway. I was a failure. With the new King in command, my life has been turned around.

The same can be true for you. In spite of poor outward circumstances, you can be a success.

27

"He's Bringing the Quilt"

There are two possible attitudes I can take toward my faults. One is to consider it too much of a chore to work on them. A second is to ignore them in the hope that they will go away, or sweep them under the rug so no one will notice them—not even me.

The alternative to these two attitudes is to make a game out of overcoming my faults. Rather than being neutralized, paralyzed, or crushed by having to face up to my flaws and shortcomings, I'm finding it can be exciting to discover what God and I, working in tandem, can do to transform my life. I can change unless I choose to remain the same. If I *choose* to grow, I believe I *will* grow.

Paul Tournier in *Guilt and Grace*[15] points out two aspects of the ministry of God through the Holy Spirit. One is to help us, God's children, see our guilt—our faults and shortcomings and the need of a savior and redeemer to transform us into what God would have us be. The other is to administer grace—to care for, comfort, and calm we children who have seen our guilt.

God never convicts us of guilt and then leaves us to suffer and reproach ourselves the rest of our lives. No, once we see the need for change, God will be the catalyst and agent for that change; the one who lets us see our guilt, but only so that we can grow from it.

I once heard about a little boy who, when asked what his favorite scripture was, answered, "Don't get excited; he's bringing the quilt." The teacher couldn't figure that one out until she finally realized the child was referring to John 16:7 (KJV): "If I depart, I will send him [the Comforter] unto you."

I am also calmed and encouraged by the ministry of the quilt or Comforter. The Holy Spirit has helped me see the guilt in my own life and also brings me comfort. I can stand to see my sins because I am seeing them in the presence of One who loves me, and who is showing them to me only for my own good.

28

Immunization

I know a distinguished medical researcher whose strong conviction is that people develop cancer as a consequence of a breakdown in the immune system that fights the disease. He believes we are all susceptible to an ever-present onslaught of cancer cells. Fortunately, most of us produce antibodies that fight those cells. When these antibodies break down, however, we are no longer able to fight the cancer, and malignancy wins the battle.

The researcher also believes stress is one of the principal causes of the breakdown of our immune system. Being upset, angry, or depressed—especially over a long period of time—tends to cause a physical as well as an emotional breakdown.

Viktor Frankl makes the same point in *Man's Search for Meaning*.[16] He tells of the death of a man who despaired when his hoped-for liberation from a concentration camp did not come. As Frankl puts it:

Those who know how close the connection is between the state of mind of a man—his courage and hope, or lack of them—and the state of immunity of his body will understand that the sudden loss of hope and courage can have a deadly effect. The ultimate cause of my friend's death was that expected liberation did not come and he was severely disappointed. This suddenly lowered his body's resistance against the latent typhus infection. His faith in the future and his will to live had become paralyzed and his body fell victim to illness.

In the last few years, more and more doctors are seeing the close correlation between our minds and our bodies. It's a vicious (or happy) circle. If our minds are not at ease, our bodies become diseased. If our bodies are diseased, this takes its toll on our minds. But if our minds are healthy and we have hope, our bodies benefit.

Most of us have seen the stress charts that actually give point ratings to distressful life events—divorce, death of a spouse, loss of a job, move to another city, and the like. If our point total is high enough, the doctors feel we are highly susceptible to a serious illness.

I'm a walking exception to the doctor's theory. I totalled my stress points one time, and they were astronomical. By all the theories I should have been dead of a heart attack, or at least should have had a bleeding ulcer or colitis. But I remained relatively healthy. Why?

I think because of Jesus Christ, I never totally lost hope. My supply was dangerously low at times, but through it all I believed Jesus Christ *could* rescue me. I'll have to be honest, though, and say I wasn't always sure he *would*. The knowledge that he could is what kept me going. That is what prevented total despair. I always had hope—my built-in immunity.

Those of us who do have faith in Christ are indeed blessed. That doesn't mean we will never fall prey to illness. We all have to die someday. As someone once said, "Life is a terminal illness."

But our chances of remaining healthy longer, having a vibrant existence, keeping our immune system intact are so much greater if we have a healthy faith. Frankl's friend in the concentration camp may not have died so soon if he had known true liberation was close at hand. It is as close as a prayer.

29

Constructive Criticism

I perhaps take criticism as poorly as anybody. I just don't like it and don't respond to it well at all. I think the reason is a self-image that is inadequate and frailer than it should be. The person who is totally self-confident (is there such a person?) would let negative criticism roll off his or her back or examine it carefully to see if it has any merit. If it does have merit, the self-confident person utilizes it and changes his or her behavior. If it doesn't, the person disregards the criticism. Those who lack self-confidence usually overreact to criticism. They become very defensive. In extreme cases they will lash out at the criticizer. How do I know? I've done it!

I think I'm growing, though. For example, I received a letter from my minister after he read the manuscript of a book I was writing. He said some very kind things about it, and gave some constructive criticism. Perhaps because of his gentle manner, because I knew he cared, because I respected him, I took to heart what he said. I re-examined the manuscript, and some things I hadn't seen before jumped out at me. He was absolutely right!

So I immediately went to work and did some major surgery on the manuscript. It was exciting to see it improved. I felt it was a vastly better work than it had been when I gave it to my friend to read. I felt much better about it.

But suppose because of our friendship or his fear of hurting my feelings, he hadn't made the comments that led to a great improvement in the book. Suppose he had simply said, "Great book, Bill," period, while having some reservations. Would he really have been my friend?

I have also been in the reverse situation. A very dear friend of mine shared with me some tapes of sermons he had preached. The content was superb, as it always is with this gifted minister. But I felt his voice needed better control. I hesitated to tell him that because I didn't want to hurt him. I believe in affirming others, not criticizing them. That's partly because I myself react so much better to affirmation than I do to criticism. But it is also because Henri Nouwen and Gordon Crosby, men I respect, write in this vein. They are great affirmers and believe we bring out people's gifts by affirming them. I also believe that with all my heart. It is a major part of my ministry.

So I struggled over whether to criticize my friend's preaching. (I wonder if the minister who wrote me about my manuscript had the same struggle.) The easy thing would have been to say nothing. Finally, I decided to give my honest opinion. I did this only because I care a great deal, because I see greatness in this man, and because I want him to be the best he can be.

What I said to him, I hope, wasn't destructive or negative criticism, but constructive criticism. I even gave him a positive suggestion about what he could do—take voice lessons, as did a well-known preacher. That man learned to modulate his voice through those lessons, and it greatly improved his oratorical ability.

There are some people who, because of their own neuroses, criticize others in the guise of "doing them a favor." I can't say I've never been guilty of this particular sin. Self-defense is a powerful motivating factor. The usual jargon is "I'm telling you this for your own good," when the real purpose (usually subconscious) is the good of the criticizer. "I just want to set the record straight" is another attack. I'm sure I've done that, and I've felt it even more than I've said it.

The criticizer relieves anxiety by blasting the other person. I suppose a criticizer could even do it in a gentle manner, although that isn't the usual approach. I think when criticism thinly veils anger, resentment, and retaliation, the adrenaline flows. Being gentle is almost impossible. At least it is that way with me. Such a criticizer doesn't evidence the love I felt in the constructive criticism from the minister who read my manuscript. That love and gentleness were undoubtedly the reason I was able to accept his advice in the spirit in which it was intended. If he had not been loving and gentle, I probably would have been defensive. I know myself too well.

If we feel compelled to speak to someone about something in a way that may smack of criticism, we should first examine our motives. Are we being constructive or destructive? How would we feel if those words were said to us, especially if they were not said with gentleness? Whose good do we really have at heart?

30

Confrontation by God

I was confronted by God through a book. Of all the books I've read through the years, this particular book spoke to me personally, at a specific time in my life, regarding specific conditions in my life.

Because of a series of "coincidences," I read a certain portion of this book on a day when I desperately needed to hear its message. The day before or the day after wouldn't have been so timely. It was as if God were right in the room with me.

The book told me exactly what I believe God would have told me if he were speaking verbally instead of through a book. The message came through loud and clear. I couldn't ignore it. I felt I was being confronted and challenged.

I also felt I was being helped, like a drowning man seeing a life preserver coming at him. I had the choice whether to reach out and accept it or to drown. It was as simple as that.

The book was *The Doctor and the Soul* by Viktor Frankl, a Jewish psychiatrist from Vienna. To my knowledge, Frankl has never professed Christianity. In his book he never directly says he believes in God. Yet he demonstrates a deep faith in God, one that seems much deeper than the superficial faith I see in some Christians. I think Frankl knows God at a very personal level. He has great insight into what life is all about. And he is directly opposed to another Viennese Jewish psychiatrist, Sigmund Freud, in one important area. Freud believed Christianity was a neurosis that must be treated and eliminated before a patient could get well. Dr. Frankl believes a deep and abiding faith in God leads to healthy, successful, and purposeful living.

What Frankl says goes against the grain of much of psychiatry and psychology, which excuses and condones, rather than confronts and challenges. We are let off the hook. We are excused because of neuroses or hang-ups not of our own doing. Our guilt is taken away, and that is supposed to bring happiness and joy. No matter how wrong we are, we are given permission to go ahead. To be happy is the goal, not to do the will of God.

Dr. Frankl talks about reverence for life, particularly with regard to suicidal or deeply depressed persons in *The Doctor and the Soul*:[17]

> Our patients can only be persuaded that life has unconditional value if we can manage to give them some content for their lives, if we can help them find an aim and a purpose in their existence—in other words, if they can be shown the task before them. . . . Nothing is more likely to

help a person overcome or endure objective difficulties or subjective troubles than the consciousness of having a task in life. That is all the more
so when the task seems to be personally cut to
suit . . . ; when it constitutes what may be called a
mission. . . . In view of the task character of life,
it logically follows that life becomes all the more
meaningful the more difficult it gets. . . . Shall we
not also test our mettle and grow in courage and
strength through the difficulties in ordinary life?

The reasoning of Jesus about loving our enemies
(Matthew 5:46) applies here as well. Just as it is easy
to love those who love us, it is also easy for us to go
through life when life is easy. There is no challenge, no
opportunity for growth. In *A Reason to Live! A Reason
to Die!*[18] John Powell says we can't say yes to God until
we have had an opportunity to say no. The person who
goes through life with everything going his or her way
is, in a sense, deprived. He or she has never had to face
up to life's difficulties and then decide whether to say
yes or no.

There are many ways of saying no to God or to life.
There are many ways out. One is suicide, the ultimate
escape. Since I have been suicidal in my life, I can speak
with some authority about that painful human condition.
It is a feeling life can't possibly hold anything good. The
present unbearable pain will last forever. There is no God
who can (and will) bring joy and meaning and purpose
back into an empty life. Romans 8:28 is not true.

All things don't work together for good. I want out, and I want out now.

But there are other cop-outs. Suicide isn't the only one. There is narcotism. Hard or soft drugs, liquor, sex, food—any of these can be wrongly used to deaden the pain.

This abuse provides a temporary escape from life, from God. It is saying to God: "I know what *you* say, but in this case, *I'm* God. I'm going to do it my way, not yours." It is saying no to God and to life. How many of us have had a chance to say no to God in these areas and have said yes? How many have had a chance to say yes and have said no?

Dr. Frankl has pinpointed a very sensitive (and therapeutic) area. He has shown us it is the attitude that matters, not the circumstances. Doesn't this go back to the very foundation of sin? After all, sin begins with attitude. Usually the attitude results in action. But even the attitude itself can be sinful. That's what Jesus was talking about in the Sermon on the Mount (Matthew 5). He also said what is in our heart and innermost being *is* us, and this can defile us (Mark 7:20, 21).

Suppose we turn the coin over and discover the problems and troubles in our lives can be opportunities for growth, for character strengthening, for improved and new attitudes. Then are we with problems in a way more blessed than those who have a relatively problem-free existence? Do we have more opportunities? Does a less than attractive man or woman have more opportunities for character strengthening and becoming more molded in the image of God than a Greek Adonis or Venus?

Gossip columns of Hollywood reporters would seem to bear this out; so would society columnists who write about the affluent and beautiful jet set. Obviously there are exceptions, but many in those spheres of life fail to demonstrate much character. Maybe it is because their lives have been too easy.

I know of a beautiful girl, from an affluent and socially prominent family, who divorced her husband when the going got tough. Someone close to her family situation, who had seen her grow up, said: "She was the Fairy Princess for whom everything was done. When trouble came, she didn't know how to handle it."

This particular young woman went for counsel to a man whose purpose was to ease her guilt feelings and help her find peace and happiness. But suppose she had gone to a therapist like Frankl who confronted her with the realities of life. Suppose instead of telling her to trust her emotions and feelings as her best and only guide, he had said: "The problems in your marriage are an opportunity. Through them you can grow into an adult, a mature human being. Instead of running from and avoiding them, why not count them as blessings—as a means to develop character, as a way to improve your attitude, as a way to say yes to God? Divorcing your husband is surely saying no. You can become a truly beautiful woman through this experience. Don't throw away your opportunity." Instead, her reaction was: "I don't *want* to commit my life to Christ. I might have to give up the divorce, and I don't want to do that."

What Frankl says in his book has revolutionized my life. I sometimes have a tendency to feel sorry for myself, to look at my problems as enemies, certainly not as friends and opportunities. That in the face of James 1:2-3 (NRSV):

> My brothers and sisters, whenever you face trials of any kind, consider it nothing but joy, because you know that the testing of your faith produces endurance.

I have a tendency to cop-out, to try to kill the pain, to wish God would immediately take away all my problems. But suppose they are left there for a purpose, to show me love and help me grow. Suppose God doesn't act like the "bellhop in the sky," that J.B. Phillips writes about in *Your God Is Too Small*? Suppose his intent is to use my problems as attitude changers? Suppose I've been singled out for a unique mission, but have to change my attitude before I can fulfill that mission? Suppose the right attitude in the midst of problems can be a "value" (Frankl's term) I can come to feel good about? Suppose I can come to feel good (but not vainly and Pharisaically proud) about my attitude? Suppose I can come to love myself more because of it?

What, then, about my problems? Are they enemies or friends, curses or opportunities? Should I blow the opportunity, or should I use it to the hilt? Should I consider it part of my mission and task in life to overcome, or should I be overcome by it?

There aren't easy solutions. All this may sound good

on paper. Living it out in the war zone called life is another matter. I believe the natural inclination is to give in. I believe wrong attitudes are our heritage, whether we call it original sin or human nature; Jesus Christ came to deliver us from them. I believe he will deliver us, provided (and what a big proviso) we say yes to God when we have the opportunity to say no.

31

Weak-Willed or Strong-Willed?

"I am weak-willed when I want to be, and when I don't want to be I'm not weak-willed," said a schizophrenic patient to Viktor Frankl. As Frankl summed it up, "This psychotic patient was skillfully pointing out that people are inclined to hide their own freedom of will from themselves by alleging weakness of will."

He also tells of a drunkard who was urged to stop drinking.

"It is already too late," he replied.
"But it is never too late."
"In that case I can quit some other time."

Frankl comments in *The Doctor and the Soul:*[19]

So long as a person makes the mistake of reminding himself constantly, before making an effort, that the effort may fail, he is not likely to succeed. . . . For example, if someone considers the possibility of cutting out drinking, he can expect all sorts of inner objections to crop up almost immediately—"But I have to" or "Still, I won't be able to resist it" and so on. If instead he simply tells himself repeatedly: "There will be no drinking—and that's all there is to it!" he will be on the right path. . . . Neurotic fatalists . . . are prone to blame childhood educational and environmental influences for "making" them what they are and having determined their destinies. These persons are attempting to excuse their weaknesses of character. . . . Neurotic fatalism is only another disguised form of escape from responsibility. . . . A faulty upbringing exonerates nobody; it has to be surmounted by conscious effort.

The choice is up to us. One of the greatest deceptions foisted on humankind is the concept of determinism, which says we can't help who we are, that we are victims of our circumstances, our environment, our upbringing, our genes.

I read in the paper some time ago about a study showing alcoholism may be inherited. Certain genetic compositions are passed on to the next generation making one person much more susceptible to alcohol addiction than another. So is the present-day alcoholic to say, "I can't help myself. My mother and father were both alcoholics. What chance do I have?" The most logical answer would simply be, "Don't drink."

I don't want to be too harsh here. I'm sure most alcoholics would say it isn't that easy. So would people driven by other compulsions. Sex is a particularly strong drive. I'm not so sure we can turn it on and off by willpower. Before we tell the homosexual "Don't do it," I think we might ask ourselves how easily we could turn off the heterosexual sex drive by willpower. Ask any man or woman who has lived alone for a long time, especially after having once been married, how tough it is. Tell such a person "Don't do it!" without being especially gentle and understanding, and you might get a fist down your throat. I'm not asking that we condone sexual acts outside marriage. I am calling for compassion and understanding. The sex life of a single adult is something I've heard few (if any) pastors speak out about. I think they are embarrassed because they don't have better answers. It's easy for them to criticize from the sanctity of their own marriage bed. I think that's the reason the wiser and more compassionate ones don't say anything. Yet they are the very ones who could be the most helpful. The abrasive judgmental ones can't be.

Just as I don't want to be too harsh (or too wishy-washy), neither do I want to be simplistic. If Frankl is wrong and sometimes our emotional instincts do wipe out our free will, then our only hope is Jesus Christ. Only he can deliver us from our passions and the bondage in which we sometimes find ourselves. Yet the pat answer, "Go pray about it," doesn't suffice either. There simply aren't any easy answers.

Frankl's form of therapy is to call people to responsible decisions and actions. His patients are confronted with responsibility for their own actions. They are not allowed to blame another person for their own inadequacies. I know of one mother who said she couldn't be a good mother to her children while married to the man to whom she was married, so she divorced him. Frankl would call that an escape, an abdication of responsibility—rationalization at its best (or worst).

I also have to contend with not taking the responsibility for my own actions. It is much easier for me to blame my failures on somebody else. But in my heart of hearts, I know I do have choices. Like the schizophrenic patient, I am also "strong-willed when I want to be, and weak-willed when I want to be." I can't honestly say, like the character named Geraldine whom comedian Flip Wilson portrayed in the 1960s, "The devil made me do it." That is usually an escape. Yet I must be aware that, in some situations, perhaps there is a kind of demonic oppression or possession that drives people and puts them in bondage. I don't think that's the usual case, though. I think, normally, we do what we *want* to do.

I also can't honestly say another person "made" me do anything I shouldn't have done. If I have done something, I have only myself to blame. I have made choices using the strong-willed side of my character and excused them by calling it weak-willed. In the final analysis I have made the choices. I did what I *wanted* to do.

If individuals in therapy could be challenged to make responsible decisions, to take responsibility for their *own* lives rather than blaming others or cutting and running when the going gets tough, they would be healthier. But far too often we see the reverse. They are encouraged to give in to their feelings, to let them happen, to seek the great god Happiness at all costs. Honor and loyalty are thrown out the window, while narcissism and self-fulfillment are welcomed with open arms. We don't really help people by letting them off the hook. We do help them by loving them and challenging them to be all they can be.

Goethe said, "If we take people as they are, we make them worse. If we treat them as if they were what they ought to be, we help them to become what they are capable of becoming."

Frankl said, "Love helps the beloved to become as the lover sees him. Live as if you were living for the second time and had acted as wrongly the first time as you are about to act now." [20]

I am speaking to myself every bit as much as I am to you. Someone once said that my writing was therapy. There's a lot in that. Sharing my thoughts, even my failings and weaknesses with you, is therapeutic. It helps me to get it all out, to give some form and substance to the convictions and beliefs I hold.

Another purpose of my writing, though, is to share with you discoveries I have made, often through great pain and hurt. I hope that through my writing, you will know you are not alone, that others share the trials and tribulations and hurts of life with you, and that there is a way through. The pain can be utilized. Hope can come to an empty life. Failure need not be ultimate. There is a Power at work in this universe that is redemptive and loving. You can tap into that Power as I have. It offers no immediate cure-all, no panacea. It doesn't take away all the pain. Problems of a lifetime don't vanish overnight. But there *is* help and love available. Isn't that enough?

32

Life Tasks

Victor Frankl's approach to counseling is very task oriented. Patients are encouraged to reject the idea that life is an unstructured ramble, that one choice is as good as another. In the last chapter I talked about Frankl's book *The Doctor and the Soul.*[21] In that book he says:

> We must also show him [the patient] that the task he is responsible for is always a specific task. . . . The task varies from person to person—in accord with the uniqueness of each person. . . . It is our business, then, to show how the life of every man has a unique goal to which only one single course leads.

Frankl could be challenged on that last sentence. Not that it isn't therapeutic to believe our lives have a unique goal. It definitely is. But I'm not sure there is only one single course leading to it. I *want* it to be so. I want God to have a special, unique plan for my life. Regardless of my failures, I want to be completely in tune with that plan.

But suppose Frankl is wrong; suppose God's only plan is to make us better, stronger, and more loving people. Does it still behoove us to cooperate with the purposes of God, to make the best of what we have, to let problems be opportunities for growth, instead of avenues for destruction and narcotism? As Puddleglum said in C. S. Lewis' tale *The Silver Chair:*[22]

> Suppose we *have* only dreamed, or made up, all those things—trees and grass and sun and moon and stars and Aslan himself. Suppose we have. Then all I can say is that, in that case, the made-up things seem a good deal more important than the real ones . . . I'm on Aslan's side even if there isn't any Aslan to lead it. I'm going to live as like a Narnian as I can even if there isn't any Narnia.

Even if God doesn't have a specific plan for my life, I still want to find one. Finding such a plan and working in conjunction with it is a much healthier way to live life than any other way I've discovered.

33

For a Reason

Whenever I hear anyone speak with assurance of what God is doing in a particular situation, it tends to make me uneasy. One night I made a hospital call with a pastor. We prayed over a sick man. The pastor said that God had made the man sick for a reason, and that if it were God's will, the man would be healed.

Another night I visited a small group meeting where I heard about the death of a month-old baby from meningitis. The young mother of that child was terminally ill with cancer. One lady said, very assuredly, that God was causing all this for a reason. Always a reason!

After the death of Pope John Paul I, I read an article about his very short papacy. It is amazing how his love and warmth captured the hearts of millions in such a short time. He certainly captured mine. Even John Paul, however, had his detractors. Some claimed God had brought about the death of this Pope for a reason. The "reason," this time, was spelled out. John Paul was "punished because he refused coronation, because he took a curious name [I thought it was a wonderful name], and because he did not try to straighten out the mess that Paul VI had made of the church." What God was doing, according to this interpretation, was "passing a negative judgment on the cardinals' decision."

Others said John Paul moved too fast and frightened some of the church hierarchy. "God does not want things to go that fast," they said. Another group, also claiming to know God's innermost thoughts, said God was "passing judgment on the arrogance of the cardinals who so confidently came out of the conclave claiming to have been personally directed by the Holy Spirit."

Kind of like the pot calling the kettle black, isn't it? Were the groups personally directed by the Holy Spirit in making these judgments?

Author Andrew Greeley summed it up well in a newspaper article:

> We humans are meaning-creating animals—"suspended in the web of meaning that we ourselves have spun." Faced with senseless and ironic tragedy, we search for meaning with far more confidence in our ability to divine the will of the ultimate powers than we should have. However, you must whistle in the dark as you pass the cemetery.

When it comes to claiming to know the secret providence of God, I draw a blank. I think I know some of what God is doing and what he demands of me. The written Word is my best guide. Claiming to know that John Paul was punished, and to know *why*, leaves me incredulous and indignant.

Maybe I'm taking the ultimate cop-out, but I'm very content to let God be God. I don't have to know or understand everything. I personally don't believe God caused my friend's illness or the death of the young baby, or that there is a purpose in the mother's cancer.

I can't explain these things. They are mysteries to me. I think they just happen in a world of free will and sin. I could be wrong. But can't we just say, "I don't know, I don't understand it, but I still love and trust God"? Do we have to determine a reason, God's reason, for every horrible thing that happens in our world?

I don't see much peace in that, or even solace for the afflicted. To think that God brings about such death and destruction can too easily lead to bitterness and resentment. We may think God's reason isn't good enough.

My plea is to let God be God and to preserve an air of mystery about many of the tragedies of our world. I realize that someday we will understand it all. Until then, let's not assign a reason to everything. I think we may ultimately find out God was also grieved over these tragedies. We may learn there was no reason or purpose at all in much of what went on in this life.

I do believe, though, God can bring good out of the worst tragedies, regardless of what or who may have caused them (or "allowed" them, as some people put it). In fact, I think one of the greatest aspects of God's majesty is to bring good out of evil. Jesus' bodily resurrection is evidence enough of that. There are "resurrections" going on all the time—resurrections of hopes and dreams, new life where hope was dead and buried.

If we look more to the possibilities that can come out of tragedy than to the cause of it, we will all be more at peace.

34

Vision Therapy

John Powell wrote an excellent book, *Fully Human, Fully Alive*,[23] in which his major premise is the way we *look* at things determines how we feel and react. As he puts it, "Emotions are always the result of a given perception and interpretation."

Powell calls this concept *vision therapy*. He says if we are to change or grow, there must first be a change in our vision or perception of reality. Our vision controls the quality of and our participation in human life. He also says our emotional reactions are not permanent parts of our makeup. Rather, they grow out of the way we see ourselves, other people, life, the world, and God. Our ideas and attitudes about these elements generate our emotional responses. Persistently negative emotions are an indication that there is distortion in our vision and our thinking, somewhat like the old verse:

Two men looked out from prison bars.
One saw mud, one saw stars.

What, then, *is* a healthy frame of reference for our lives?

What is the vision that will make us whole? Powell says:

> Everyone must learn to believe in someone or
> something so deeply that life is charged with
> meaning and a sense of mission. And the more
> one dedicates oneself to this meaning and mis-
> sion, the more such a person will develop a sense
> of profound and personal belonging and discover
> the reality of community. . . . It is a matter of
> commitment to a person or a cause in which one
> can believe and to which one can be directed.[24]

The vision, the frame of reference that can make us
whole is Jesus Christ. He is the person or cause to whom
we can be dedicated.

35

Becoming a Person

I once attended a conference of European doctors concerned with medicine for the whole person. They believe in order to properly take care of their patients, they must help meet emotional and spiritual needs as well as strictly physical ones. They believe many physical symptoms are the result of emotional and/or spiritual problems.

While attending that conference, I read a book called *The Age of Sensation*[25] by Herbert Hendin, an American psychiatrist and psychoanalyst. I couldn't help seeing a dark contrast between the persons Hendin was writing about and a "whole person." Hendin did an extensive study of American college students of the mid-1970s, and thought the attitudes and symptoms he recognized in the study were creeping into the mainstream of American life. He saw a vast change from just twenty years before the study. What he found was general disillusionment and lack of purpose, which he described as follows:

> This culture is marked by a self-interest and ego-centrism that increasingly reduces all relations to

the question: What am I getting out of it? Nothing blocks involvement more effectively than a sense that anything felt or done for another person is a wearisome burden or that nothing is worthwhile that does not immediately result in some gain. . . . For both sexes in this society, caring deeply for anyone is becoming synonymous with losing. Men seem to want to give women less and less, while women increasingly see demands men make as inherently demeaning.

Contrast this with a remark made by a psychologist at the European conference of doctors and counselors, most of whom were Christians: "Becoming a person is loving and being loved by somebody." Another doctor there said, "Love is the challenge of the gospel. It's love that gives meaning to all of life."

The young people Dr. Hendin writes about had no meaning in their lives. They had no purpose other than to hide their emotions for fear of being hurt. They have been terribly damaged by a society that puts such stress on personal ambition and *self*-fulfillment.

I know of only one way that suffering from meaninglessness can be relieved. It is by helping people take a 180-degree turn from narcissism and *self*-centeredness to a concern for Jesus Christ. That, in turn, will enable them to not only love themselves, but others as well. Then they can be whole persons—who love and are loved by others.

36

What Is Wholeness?

Wholeness is having a healthy self-image. At least that's the key, a place to start growing. Without a healthy self-image, there is no way we can be whole.

A poor self image inflicts so much destruction and havoc on a person. I once talked to a friend who told me about a woman he worked with. She was a very nice person, he said, but had a horrible self-image. She went around with her head hanging down, sure in her own mind that she was worthless and would make mistakes. So she did.

In so many ways, we are prisoners of our own minds. If we think we are worthless, we usually act that way. If we think we have real merit, we usually end up doing meritorious things. We certainly can't call a person whole who goes around thinking ill of him- or herself. On the other hand, I wouldn't call a person whole who had an exaggerated opinion of self and his or her own abilities. Nothing is more unpalatable than conceit. But I think that conceitedness is often a mask for deep-rooted feelings of insecurity and inferiority—again, a poor self-image.

If wholeness is a healthy self-image, how do we acquire it? I think there's only one way, and that is to be loved, genuinely loved for who we are rather than for what we *do*. Yet we are all loved with a love like that. We are loved by Someone who loves us with a love whose depths we can't begin to fathom. Some of us have seen a lot of that love in our lives. We've seen God at work loving us. Even so, I still think we've only scratched the surface in our understanding of it.

But as crucial as that love is, and although in some cases that love alone is enough to sustain us, most of us seem to need human love as well for wholeness and a healthy self-image. Outside of God's love, nothing is as regenerative as human love in building a healthy feeling of self-worth.

As I have said before, we are not placed on this earth to see through each other, but to see each other through. How seldom we see this in action! How often we are so busily engaged in seeing through other people that we have little time, inclination, or desire to see them through.

37

Self-Defense and Self-Love

As e. e. cummings once wrote: "To be nobody but yourself in a world which is doing its best, night and day, to make you everybody else, means to fight the hardest battle which any human being can fight; and never stop fighting." So many people won't let us be ourselves. We have to be somebody else to be loved, appreciated, accepted. But unless we are loved, how can we be ourselves? How can we even be lovable if no one loves us?

To put it in the words of Thomas Merton: "There is no way under the sun of making man worthy of love except by loving him." When we aren't loved, when we aren't accepted for who we are, we have a tendency to become defensive. And a defensive person is not a very lovable person.

An acquaintance of mine has written a fable reminiscent of Hannah Hurnard's *Hind's Feet on High Places*. In the fable God explains some intricacies of the human personality, it seems to me, quite accurately. God says, "Humans need to feel they are lovable and acceptable. Then they don't have to spend so much energy defending themselves."

I have spent far too much energy defending myself against what I believed were false assessments about me and my motives. I am sure this was because I was not secure enough in my assessment of myself. It was also because I had not trusted God enough to give the *justification* I felt I needed. (Perhaps *wanted* would be a more accurate term than *needed.*) When we really get down to it, why is any justification needed? If I am right with God—through his grace, not my efforts—then I am more likely to be able to feel, as well as say, that old childhood proverb "Sticks and stones may break my bones, but names can never hurt me."

It is wonderful, though, to have human love as well as God's love. I have had both, and they have helped me feel more lovable. Love has encouraged me to become less defensive—but I'm not totally there yet. I'm still struggling.

38

Through Another's Eyes

One New Year's Eve I was jammed into Preservation Hall in New Orleans trying to watch and listen to a Dixieland jazz concert. I did more listening than watching, for the sea of humanity in front of me prevented my getting a good view.

My daughter, who is six inches shorter than I, was with me. About all she saw was people's backs. She just wasn't tall enough to see over the crowd. Sensing her plight and wanting to see what she saw, I bent down so I was about her height. Sure enough, backs were all there was to see.

This experience gave me an insight. We so seldom try to see what the other person sees. Perhaps we can look over the heads of the crowd, but our friend or neighbor is limited to a view of backs. We may have our life relatively put together and see bright skies. Our neighbor is suffering and sees only dark clouds.

All of us would be both more humane and empathic persons if we would at least try to see life from another person's viewpoint. That doesn't mean we have to agree with someone's actions, but we can at least make an effort to understand. I suspect if we had the same upbringing—or the same misfortunes—we might see life the same way the other person does. And our actions might not be all that different.

We are so quick to judge, when "but for the grace of God, there go I." And we are more comfortable avoiding the look through another's eyes. That might cause us to change our perspective, our viewpoint, our attitude; and we don't want to do that.

In that same mob scene at the concert was a little Chinese girl no more than seven or eight years old. If all my daughter could see was backs, then all this little girl could see was knees. I offered to pick her up and hold her so that she could see from my vantage point—or even higher. But she refused. I suspect she was frightened of a total stranger and didn't understand my intentions.

Her response led me to another insight. Sometimes we who cannot see are too frightened to let another person help us. We don't know what is in store for us if we become vulnerable and let another "lift us up" to higher ground. We remain locked into a view of knees and backs when we could be seeing mountaintops if we only ventured forth in faith.

Jesus Christ is here to lift us up, but so often we refuse. We are afraid. We are more comfortable with backs and knees. There is so much out there to see in this world if we would but look at it through another person's eyes and let Christ give us his vantage point. I hope we don't limit ourselves by a refusal to see.

39

Our Redeemer Lives

I have read Romans 7 many times—the part where Paul tells about doing the things he knows he shouldn't, and not doing the things he should. I have also read the part where he asks, "Who on earth can set me free from the clutch of my own sinful nature?" The answer, of course, is Jesus Christ.

I've struggled with these passages because I have been so aware of my failures and the many times I have not done what I ought. I also know Paul was writing about his experiences *after* becoming a Christian. No recounting of preconversion experiences here. Paul is describing the Christian life *as it is*—not only his life, but mine.

As many times as I read these passages, the obvious insight of what the victory is all about always escaped me. I could relate to the failures; I couldn't relate to the victory on a once-and-for-all basis. I have had victories—but I never could maintain them. I always fell back into my old ways.

Finally, though, I received the insight that I think is

there. I believe the Lord showed it to me at a particular time when I desperately needed it. Jesus did not speak to me audibly, but these are the words that were impressed upon my spirit. I believe they express what Paul was trying to convey in Romans 8, when he talks about the victory that can be achieved in and through Jesus Christ.

Bill, the victory is *not* once-and-for-all. That is what you have been looking for, but you will never find it. What I will do is restore you and lift you up each time you fall down. *That* is how I will deliver you. You can never lose my love. I will never fail you. I will lift you up.

What a relief to finally see this. Someone told me once that I had blown it and that it was too late. But that's not true. With God it is *never* too late. There is no way we can blow it. Fail, yes. That is precisely what Paul is telling us we *will* do. But he is also saying we have a deliverer *each and every time we fail.* If we didn't, our sins would do ultimate harm. If we failed once—as we all do—there would be no redemption. But there is redemption because, as Job put it, our Redeemer lives.

Epilogue

A Love That Will Not Let Me Go

Some reviewers of my first book, *Joy Comes with the Morning*, were kind enough to say I evidenced love for my readers. I hope that was so. I know I felt it. But in concluding this book on hope, I want to write about another kind of love—not our love for other people, but God's love for us, an ever-faithful love that has given me hope in times of great despair. It has sustained me and kept me going in times when I literally had no other hope. At such times, I felt God's love; I sensed it; I knew it was there. It is a love that cannot be measured by human standards. It sets us free. Yet at the same time it will not let us go.

While I was writing this book, I felt this love more strongly than I have ever felt it before. I knew God would never stop loving me, *no matter what I did.* I couldn't have driven God away if I had tried—and in some ways I did try, or at least tested that love to the extreme. I found God ever faithful, always ready to forgive, always willing to help and to instill hope.

I have one more thought to explore with you in this book. If you can accept it as truth, can let it seep into

your psyche and inner being, then you will have hope. It
may be the most important thing I'll ever have to say to
any of my readers.

I am indebted to John Claypool, an Episcopal priest,
for this final illustration. He preached a sermon titled
"Surprise Is God's Other Name." In it he told the story of
Abraham—a man given a promise by God. But Abraham
was a man who didn't always walk in that promise. He
didn't trust God enough to let God accomplish the special purposes of Abraham's life and keep that promise.

If there were ever a man like Abraham, it has been
me. I'm not talking about the Abraham who, because of
his great faith in God, laid his own son Isaac on the sacri-
ficial block. I don't think I could have done that. I'm
talking about the Abraham who ran off to Egypt to find
his own food because he didn't trust God to continue
providing. I'm talking about the Abraham who thought
he knew how to provide, in another way, the heir God
had promised, since his own wife was too old to have
children.

When I say I have been like Abraham, I mean I have
not trusted God sufficiently. I have sometimes laughing-
ly said (yet, down deep, probably meant it), "The Holy
Spirit needs my help. I'll just move things along a little
by my own efforts." One flagrant example of this is
that, while claiming to believe that only the Holy Spirit
can bring anyone to a commitment to Christ, I have
usurped that role in trying by my own efforts to bring
someone very dear to me to personal faith in Christ.
And my motives have not been unselfish. I wanted that

commitment because of what it would do for *me*, not for the other person.

Every time I have tried to "help" God along, I've muddied up the water and possibly delayed the fulfillment of some of God's promises. I have *said* I believed and trusted, but I have only given lip service to my belief. If I had truly believed, if my life had been truly committed to Christ, I would have taken my hands off and let God fulfill those promises. God's way and timing are not mine.

Claypool's sermon gave me new hope. It made me realize afresh, and in a more powerful way than ever before, that God is a promise-keeper. He *will* act—even in very surprising ways. Let me quote from the sermon.

> When you come in contact with the God depicted in the Bible, you might as well get ready for surprises, because the truth of the matter is, "His ways are not as our ways, nor are his thoughts as our thoughts." . . . [God] made specific enough promises but then went about fulfilling them in totally unprecedented ways. [He] could always be depended upon but never anticipated precisely.
>
> Abraham was to learn to do two things—to obey this God and then trust him to bring it to pass; to believe in the One who was doing the promising, and to follow instructions step by step and allow him to fulfill things as he would. Learning to obey and trust this kind of God was a high challenge indeed. It involved unwavering trust in the content of the promises, but also wide latitude

as to the forms the fulfillment would take—being certain that God will keep his word, but uncertain as to how and when and by what means all of this would come to pass.

Our tendency is to set limits on reality according to our perceptions; to create a set of expectations out of our past experiences and then judge everything by them rather than making room for wonder and surprise. What we need to do is realize that God is the only adequate predicate for words like *possible* or *impossible*. Who are we to speak dogmatically about what can and cannot be?

How can we ever set limits on him or dare to reduce him down to our pathetic images of what is possible or impossible? Yet we do this—again and again we embrace despair about the future or this or that situation and decide ahead of time that nothing can be done. . . . Nathaniel [when he said, "No good thing could come out of Nazareth"] was superimposing his vision of the possible on the One "who can make the things that are out of the things that are not, and who can make dead things come alive again." How mistaken can one be?

What has been is most emphatically not the full measure of what can be. Letting the past totally dominate the future is something one has no right to do wherever the God of the Bible is concerned.

. . . Thus the challenge is to learn to trust and to obey, confident that he will keep his word, but flexible as to when and how and in what form he will do it. About the only thing you can safely expect is that what he will do will not be what you expected—rather something bigger and better and vaster than you ever dreamed. The worst sin of all against this kind of God is the sin of despair—to label as "impossible" some "Nazareth" and say, "No good can ever come out of here." The truth of the matter is: *Good did come*—out of Nazareth and Sarah and thousands of other unlikely places, and if this be so, who are you to give up hope on your life or your circumstances or your future? With that kind of God despair is presumptuous. It is concluding something about the future you have no right to conclude. Who knows what this God of surprises can bring out of the day-by-day events of your life?

"Who knows what this God of surprises can bring out of the day-by-day events of your life?" Let the hope and possibility of those words sink deep into our minds. We do indeed have a God who acts, a God who loves. And we have seen God's love personified in Jesus of Nazareth. That love is still here for us today. I can personally testify to it because I have experienced it. That is the reason I have joy. That is the reason I have hope.

Jesus Christ can be your hope and your joy as well. As John Claypool says, "Let it be, O God of surprises, let it be."

Notes

Chapter 4
1. Irvin D. Yalom, *The Theory and Practice of Group Psychotherapy* (New York: Basic Books, 1970).
2. Eugene Kennedy, *The Pain of Being Human* (Chicago: Thomas More Press, 1972).

Chapter 8
3. Kathryn Lindskoog, *The Lion of Judah in Never–Never Land* (Grand Rapids: William B. Eerdmans Publishing Co., 1973).
4. George MacDonald, *The Princess and the Goblin* (New York: Dutton, 1949).
5. C. S. Lewis, *The Weight of Glory* (New York: Macmillan, 1949).

Chapter 12
6. Elizabeth O'Connor, *Call to Commitment* (New York: Harper & Row, 1963).
7. C. S. Lewis, *The Magician's Nephew* (New York: Macmillan, 1955).

Chapter 14
8. Catherine Mashall, *Adventures in Prayer* (Boston: G. K. Hall & Co., 1975).

Chapter 15
9. Paul Tournier, *Guilt and Grace* (New York: Harper & Row, 1962).
10. Tournier, *Guilt and Grace.*

Chapter 16
11. Tournier, *Guilt and Grace.*
12. Tournier, *Guilt and Grace.*

Chapter 21
    13. Earl Palmer, *Salvation by Surprise* (Waco, TX: Word, 1975).

Chapter 26
    14. George Vaillant, *Adaptation to Life* (Boston: Little, Brown, 1977).

Chapter 27
    15. Tournier, *Guilt and Grace*.

Chapter 28
    16. Viktor Frankl, *Man's Search for Meaning* (Boston: Beacon Press, 1963).

Chapter 30
    17. Viktor Frankl, *The Doctor and the Soul* (New York: Random House, 1973).
    18. John Powell, *A Reason to Live! A Reason to Die!* (Allen, TX: Argus Communications, 1972).

Chapter 31
    19. Frankl, *The Doctor and the Soul*.
    20. Frankl, *The Doctor and the Soul*.

Chapter 32
    21. Frankl, *The Doctor and the Soul*.
    22. C. S. Lewis, *The Silver Chair* (New York: Macmillan, 1955).

Chapter 34
    23. John Powell, *Fully Human, Fully Alive* (Niles, IL: Argus Communications, 1976).
    24. Powell, *Fully Human, Full Alive*.

Chapter 35
    25. Herbert Hendin, *The Age of Sensation* (New York: W. W. Norton, 1975).

Stephen Ministries

Stephen Ministries is a not-for-profit Christian training and educational organization founded in 1975 and based in St. Louis, Missouri. Its mission is:

> To equip the saints for the work of ministry, for building up the body of Christ, until all of us come to the unity of the faith and of the knowledge of the Son of God, to maturity, to the measure of the full stature of Christ.
>
> *Ephesians 4:12–13*

The 40-person staff of Stephen Ministries carries out this mission by developing and delivering high-quality, Christ-centered training and resources to:

- help congregations and other organizations equip and organize people to do meaningful ministry; and
- help individuals grow spiritually, relate and care more effectively, and live out their faith in daily life.

Stephen Ministries is best known for the Stephen Series system of lay caring ministry, but it also offers resources in many other areas, including grief support, assertiveness, spiritual gifts, ministry mobilization, caring evangelism, church antagonism, and inactive member ministry.

A number of these resources are described on the following pages. To learn more about these and other resources or to order them, contact us at:

 Stephen Ministries
2045 Innerbelt Business Center Drive
St. Louis, Missouri 63114-5765
(314) 428-2600
www.stephenministries.org

The Stephen Series

 The Stephen Series is a complete system for training and organizing laypeople to provide one-to-one Christian care to hurting people in the congregation and community.

Stephen Leaders—pastors, staff, and lay leaders—are trained to begin and lead Stephen Ministry in the congregation.

Stephen Leaders, in turn, equip and supervise a team of Stephen Ministers—congregation members who provide ongoing care and support to people experiencing grief, divorce, hospitalization, terminal illness, unemployment, loneliness, and other life difficulties.

As a result:

- hurting people receive quality care during times of need;
- laypeople use their gifts in meaningful ministry;
- pastors no longer are expected to personally provide all the care that people need; and
- the congregation grows as a more caring community.

More than 11,000 congregations and organizations from more than 150 denominations—from across the United States, Canada, and 24 other countries—have enrolled in the Stephen Series so they can more effectively provide Christ-centered care to people in need.

Journeying through Grief

Journeying through Grief is a set of four short books that individuals, congregations, and other organizations can share with grieving people at  four crucial times during the first year after a loved one has died.

Book 1: *A Time to Grieve,* sent three weeks after the loss

Book 2: *Experiencing Grief,* sent three months after the loss

Book 3: *Finding Hope and Healing,* sent six months after the loss

Book 4: *Rebuilding and Remembering,* sent eleven months after the loss

Each book focuses on the feelings and issues the person is likely to be experiencing at that point in their grief, offering reassurance, encouragement, and hope. In *Journeying through Grief,* Kenneth Haugk writes in a warm, caring style. He shares from the heart, drawing on his personal and professional experience and from the insights of many others. The books provide a simple yet powerful way to express ongoing concern to a bereaved person throughout the difficult first year.

Each set comes with four mailing envelopes and a tracking card that makes it easy to know when to send each book.

Also available is a *Giver's Guide* containing suggestions for using the books as well as sample letters that can be personalized and adapted to send with them.

Don't Sing Songs to a Heavy Heart:
How to Relate to Those Who Are Suffering

Pastors, lay caregivers, and suffering people alike have high praise for *Don't Sing Songs to a Heavy Heart* by Kenneth Haugk, a warm and practical resource for what to do and say to hurting people in times of need.

Forged in the crucible of Dr. Haugk's own suffering and grief, *Don't Sing Songs to a Heavy Heart* draws from his personal experience and from extensive research with more than 4,000 other people.

For anyone who has ever felt helpless in the face of another person's pain, *Don't Sing Songs to a Heavy Heart* offers practical guidance and common-sense suggestions for how to care in ways that hurting people welcome—while avoiding the pitfalls that can add to their pain.